IMPRINT

© 2024 Federico Maffini. All rights reserved.

First Edition, September 2024

Published by Federico Maffini
through Amazon Kindle Direct Publishing

ISBN: 9798332301681 (Paperback)

This book is a work of non-fiction. The opinions expressed are the author's own and do not necessarily reflect the views of any individuals or organizations mentioned.

No part of this book may be reproduced, distributed, or transmitted in any form or by any means, including photocopying, recording, or other electronic or mechanical methods, without the prior written permission of the author, except in the case of brief quotations embodied in critical reviews and certain other non-commercial uses permitted by copyright law.

For permissions requests, please contact: federico.maffini@gmail.com

Cover design by: Federico Maffini
Edited by: Federico Maffini

ZERO BULLSH*T PROGRAM MANAGEMENT

THE ZERO TO HERO PROGRAM MANAGEMENT PLAYBOOK:

A BLUEPRINT TO MASTERING PROGRAM MANAGEMENT

Federico Maffini

To those who helped me along the way, shared their knowledge, and trusted me with bigger and bolder projects. To those who saw the person I wanted to be when I grew up and chiselled it out of a block of raw material.

To my family, cheering for me from the land of Parma ham and Parmesan cheese.

To Eleonora, whose resilience, dedication, commitment, and sheer ambition pushed me beyond my own limits time and again. I will never stop learning from her.

TABLE *of* CONTENTS

Preface 1

    What This Book Is and What It Is Not 4

    Who This Book Is For.. 5

    Program vs Product vs Project Management............... 6

        Bonus: Portfolio Managers................................. 13

        Bonus: Real-life Program and Product Management 13

A Blueprint for Repeatable Program Management......17

    Step 1 - Setting Things Up: The Program's Charter.. 19

    Step 2 - Building: What Success Looks Like............. 26

        Mechanize: Remove Best Intentions 27

        Measure: Metrics, Goals and KPIs 31

        Manage: Stakeholder Management..................... 40

    Step 3 - Branching Out: Beyond Your Program 50

        Pilots & Experiments 50

        Delivering Through Others.................................. 56

        Building a High-Functioning Team: Beyond The Basics 58

    Step 4 - Wrapping Things Up: Happy and Not-So-Happy Endings 63

        Happy Endings 64

        Not-so-Happy Endings 68

Generative AI For Program Management 71

    The Foundations 72

        Types of Artificial Intelligence 72

        Rapid-fire GenAI Jargon 73

        A Few GenAI Myths To Bust 75

    GenAI-augmented Program Management 77

Closing 80

Fed's corner 85

    One Interview like a STAR 86

    Two Storytelling in Program Management 90

    Three Managers without borders 94

    Four Escalating sucks, until it doesn't 98

    Five Say NO to your manager 103

Frequently Asked Questions 107

    FAQ 1: How do I strike the right balance between challenging and realistic goals? 107

    FAQ 2. What alternatives do I have to Outlook email updates? 110

    FAQ 3. What's the difference between A/B testing and running a pilot? 111

    FAQ 4: How do I balance multiple programs simultaneously? 112

    FAQ 5: How do I handle scope creep in a program? 114

    FAQ 6: What's the best approach for transitioning a successful pilot into a full-scale program? 115

Appendices **117**

    Appendix 1: Writing a good executive summary 117

    Appendix 2: Sample tenets from real-life examples 119

    Appendix 3: Other examples of mechanisms 120

    Appendix 4: More on stakeholder management: Stakeholder Mapping 121

    Appendix 5. GenAI-augmented PMs, A Day in the Life 122

    Appendix 6. Outlook email templates 133

PREFACE

"Hey, I'm Federico. I'm originally from Italy. I've been in the UK for the past six years and, before that, I was in Luxembourg. Ever heard of Luxembourg? No? You're not missing out. It's a tiny place in the heart of Europe with not a whole lot going on there—except advantageous tax rates..."

Chances are, if you've ever been in an introductory meeting with me, you've heard those exact same lines. That's how I usually kick things off whenever someone asks me to introduce myself. New mentees, new colleagues, new managers. Then, depending on the purpose of the call, I continue with something along these lines:

"I started my career at Amazon as an intern. My university in the Netherlands required me to do an internship to graduate, so I applied to dozens of companies all across Europe. When Amazon reached out, I didn't even remember I had applied for a role there. The catch? The internship was in Finance, the only job I was sure I hated. Maths, statistics, accounting - I despised it all. What I really wanted to do at the time was marketing, guerrilla campaigns, and viral advertising. But how could I possibly turn down a role at Amazon?

So, there I was, studying Excel through YouTube videos, researching interview questions on Glassdoor.com, and feeling incapable of learning SQL in the few weeks I had before my interview round. Then the day finally came. I rented a car, embarked on a 300 km drive from the Netherlands to Luxembourg (at the time Amazon interviewed everyone in person and on-site), and gave everything I had in what truly was my first ever real job interview. The rest is history."

At Amazon, time seemed to fly. I truly loved being part of the company and I soaked it all up like a sponge: the culture, the leadership principles, the peculiar ways of working, the customer obsession, everything. My career progressed rapidly, with two promotions in Finance and two more after leaving it behind. Despite knowing Finance wasn't my long-term career aspiration, my years across Amazon Transportation Controllership and Amazon Transportation Finance were extremely formative, and I'll be forever grateful for the opportunity. I learned how to be a Finance/Data Analyst surrounded by people who made me feel dumb every day (in the most positive way!) and I was moulded to think analytically even in the least data-driven contexts – a skill that has proven fundamental time and again as a Program Manager and business leader. It's something anyone should invest time in perfecting as early on in their career as possible.

As I closed that chapter and moved on to program management, it became clear to me that my analytical upbringing and habit of bridging actuals vs plan would be useful even when discussing customer experience and customer sentiment. This shift marked a pivotal moment in my personal and professional development. For the first time, I realised that I did have transferable skills that I could rely on when facing new, ambiguous challenges in unfamiliar contexts.

From there, I went on to manage larger teams, lead other leaders, and expand my scope progressively alongside, and with the unwavering support of, some of the most inspirational leaders you can ever come across.

In more recent times, I started mentoring other professionals who do not have the luxury of a robust mentoring system within their own companies and feel they could use some guidance and expertise. Mentoring was, and still is, extremely formative for me and the actual catalyst for writing this book. It gave me confidence that what I know and have to say does matter, can help others, and that I should not take it for granted. It made me realise how lucky I have been to have had the support system I had around me. It made me a better leader and a better person all around, and that is what I want to pass on to others too.

This book – or anthology rather – is just that: a collection of everything I have learned throughout the years that has helped and shaped me personally and professionally. It's my way of helping others fast-track their path to program management by providing practical advice and insights. It's practical, concise, and, hopefully, helpful.

What This Book Is and What It Is Not

"Clear is Kind and Unclear is Unkind". First reported by writer and Professor Brené Brown, at its essence, this mantra emphasizes the importance of clear communication in fostering trust and connection. When we're clear with our words and intentions, we show respect for others' time and emotions.

So, let me be crystal clear (and extra kind):

What this book is:

- A mix of diary entries, collected notes, and first-hand experiences I've gathered throughout the years and the many hours of mentoring I've delivered.
- What I wish someone had told me, or explained to me, earlier on.
- A catalyst for more offline discussions, conversations, and research.
- Something I mainly wrote for myself and in my spare time because I truly enjoy the process.
- An attempt to make my mum proud: she's always wanted me to be a writer, after all.

What this book is not:

- A schoolbook, a course, or a textbook. And I am not a professor.
- A comprehensive manual on what Program, Project, or Product management is or isn't. Boring.
- The new Harry Potter or The Lord of the Rings. "Writing stuff" and "being a writer" are two very different things,

and I know where my place is. That said, I did do my best to make it an interesting and well-formulated read.
- A regurgitation of GenAI or plagiarised content. I did virtually no research to write what's here, as my primary intent was to document my own learnings and experience. After all, Google is free... use it!

Who This Book Is For

Anyone eager to understand what Program Management is.
Anyone looking for tips & tricks on Program Management.
Anyone about to, or on the precipice of, becoming a PM.
Anyone gravitating around Biz Ops & Management.
Anyone feeling they need extra info on PM.
Anyone with PM in their title.
Anyone curious.
Anyone??
Anyone!

Whether you're on the brink of stepping into the role of a Program Manager or already deep in the trenches, this book will hopefully have something for you. However, as we all know, there's rarely a one-size-fits-all approach in business, and program management is no exception. Even though some parts of this book might seem obvious to seasoned pros, and others might feel a bit too advanced or inapplicable to others, that's okay. The beauty of program management is its diversity and versatility, and this book was written with that in mind. All I hope for is that all readers will be able to walk away with something they can implement in their day-to-day right away.

If you do, please do let me know! I would love to hear some first-hand feedback to ensure I haven't just wasted the last 6 months of my life :)

Now, before we dive in, let me set the stage for the central theme of this book: Program Management and its interconnected elements.

Program vs Product vs Project Management

Four years and a couple of promotions in, I knew my 20-year plan wasn't to be the CFO at the boardroom table. I wanted to move closer to the business and to the actual customers. Most importantly, I wanted to be the one making decisions on behalf of the business I was part of. True, finance leaders have as much weight in a lot of the decision-making as their business counterparts, but on a day-to-day basis, and especially at more junior levels, the work of a business person is ultimately what I wanted for myself.

As I started to look and apply for internal roles, I explored a wide array of possibilities: marketing (hit YouTube and type: "Donny for a Smile" for a glimpse into *what it could have been*), business analytics, account management, and obviously, program management. Now, I could lie and say I was passionate about program management all along for some grander reason, but I wasn't. The only thing I knew was that Program Managers within the Amazon Kindle department (where I interned at the start of my career) were the ones coordinating the launch of new products (new Kindle e-readers, Alexa devices, etc.) and that seemed pretty cool. I remember they would throw launch parties whenever something big went to market, or meet in the office in the middle of the night to follow the launch in some overseas market. That's what drew me in, and that's all I knew at the time.

So much so that I proceeded with the assumption that all PM roles (Program Management, Product Management, and Project Management) would be the same and would get me where I wanted to go. Wrong. Very wrong.

Unsurprisingly, it took me months to transition away from finance and into a business role, possibly because I was approaching hiring managers for Senior PM roles saying something along the lines of *"I'd love to move closer to the business and to the customers and that's why I'm looking for a PM role. Whether Program, Product or Project Management, it doesn't really matter to me"*. Not very smart of me. But hey, we are all here to learn!

It was only when I became an actual Program Manager and started to work with an actual (and way more experienced) Product Manager that I finally understood the difference between all these roles. Let me help you avoid the same mistakes with some self-informed, partial, and unofficial definitions. For anything more academic and detailed, remember: Google is your friend.

Product Managers. Product management guides every step of a product's lifecycle, from development to positioning and pricing, by focusing on the product and its customers first and foremost. Product Managers are orchestrators. They inform their product roadmaps by working backwards from their customers (whether internal to the company or external), and then partner closely with technical teams (software development managers and their teams of engineers) to build the right products and features. In short, they worry about everything needed to build, launch, and maintain a product – from user experience to user interface, from product bugs to ongoing feature requests, from go-to-market strategies and more. If I were to summarize the typical skills of the Product Managers I interfaced with, those would be:

- **Customer focus**: Deep understanding of customer needs and the ability to translate them into product features. This includes gathering and integrating customer feedback to continually improve the product.
- **Roadmap planning**: Capability to develop and communicate a clear product roadmap that aligns with business goals.
- **Technical understanding**: In-depth knowledge of the technical aspects surrounding product delivery, enabling effective collaboration with engineering teams.
- **Priority management**: Ability to prioritize features and initiatives based on customer impact and business value, often in constrained environments with scarce technical capacity.
- **Go-to-Market strategy**: Proficiency in planning and executing product launches, including marketing and sales strategies, user experience design principles, legal and compliance considerations, and more.

Project Managers. Project Managers ensure their projects get delivered on time, on budget, and to the satisfaction of their customer/s, whether internal or external to the company. They are mostly Individual Contributors (ICs) and often work with a pool of stakeholders across all parts of the business. Two things are unique about Project Managers: first, they usually have a very clear and specific, time-bound project (a goal basically) to achieve. Picture the launch of a new production plant by the end of the year, the offshoring of certain activities to a third-party provider by the end of the quarter, the transformation of the tech stack within a specific department by next week, etc. Second, budgeting and resource management are often (always?) big parts of their job, which does not always apply to Program and Product Managers. As far as their typical skills, this is what I've observed first-hand:

- **Planning and scheduling**: Expertise in developing detailed project plans and timelines that are easy for others to understand and follow.
- **Resource management**: Ability to allocate resources efficiently across the group of stakeholders, and manage budgets effectively.
- **Time management**: Unparalleled ability to manage time effectively to ensure project milestones are met.
- **Risk management and problem-solving**: Proficiency in identifying, assessing, and mitigating project risks, with a strong ability to resolve issues that arise during the project lifecycle.
- **Communication**: Clear and consistent communication with project teams and stakeholders.

Program Managers. Theoretically, Program Managers should operate at a more strategic level than Project Managers as programs should encompass various projects, and it would not be uncommon for Project Managers to report into a Program Manager. In practice, I am yet to come across an example where this structure is rigorously followed. However, Program management remains the most versatile, most strategic, and most cross-functional profile amongst all of the "Pro*** Management" roles. Often, Program and Product Managers work very closely too, with the two splitting the responsibilities within a larger space.

For example, in Amazon Shipping I owned everything to do with Customer Experience and Customer Support from a programmatic standpoint, and I was working very closely with a Product Manager who owned the delivery of new technical products within the Customer Support space. He would come to me to know the long-term plan for the charter (i.e., we want Customer Support to look like this in the future) and he would then build the product vision to get us there (i.e., for Customer Support to look like *that*, we need *so* and *so* product feature and *this* is how we will go about building and launching everything).

However, in Amazon Web Services, I led teams of Program Managers that did not pair up with any Product Manager as their scope was specific to go-to-market motions and internal strategic initiatives. For example, we want X team (Sales team) to own Y initiative (prevent customers from churning) to achieve Z result (protect $1M in revenue), and this is everything we need to do to get there (telemetry, enablement, monthly mechanisms, goals, KPIs, etc.).

Looking back on my own journey and those of far better PMs I've crossed paths with, these are some common traits:

- **Leadership, influencing without authority**: Pronounced ability to inspire and guide cross-functional teams towards a common goal, often without any formal authority over others.
- **Strategic thinking**: Capability to see the big picture and align program goals with higher organisational objectives.
- **Communication**: Proficiency in conveying complex ideas clearly to stakeholders at all levels. Also, key is the ability to speak the language of more/less technical stakeholders and customers. Ultimately, Program Managers are bridges between groups of stakeholders.
- **Analytical skills**: Competence in analysing data to drive decision-making and measure Program success. This easily translates to Product and Project Managers too, but Program Managers tend to handle more varied and complex spaces and are responsible for a wider set of goals, metrics, and KPIs. Diving deep on actual vs plan performance is also often within their responsibility, even when paired with a Product Manager.
- **Problem-solving**: Ability to identify issues quickly and develop effective solutions across a variety of workstreams and competing priorities.
- **Stakeholder Management**: Skill in engaging and managing stakeholders, ensuring their needs and expectations are met.

Navigating the transition from Finance to Program Management was a challenging but rewarding journey. I could tell you that "it required a lot of self-reflection, learning, and persistence as well as understanding my own strengths and weaknesses, aligning my career goals with my personal passions, and continuously seeking out opportunities to develop new skills". But in reality, none of that is true. I did not network as I should have, I did not dive deep on each of the roles, and I did not spend time studying the nuances of the path I was so sure I wanted to undertake.

However, there is a key lesson I took away and that has remained true for my career thus far: the importance of **adaptability**. The business landscape is constantly evolving and the level of uncertainty is always high, especially in fast-growing, ever-evolving industries. Being able to adapt to new challenges and rise to opportunities is essential for our own long-term success, and so is the resilience to push through uncertainty time and again. We will never know everything and we will never be able to make perfect choices – what we ought to do though is to remain curious and willing to learn and explore. Ultimately, taking calculated risks is necessary for self-growth and moving horizontally in a company that allows you to do so is the greatest (non-monetary) benefit you could ever hope to get.

For those who find themselves at a career crossroads, unsure which path to take, my advice is to stay curious, be proactive, and seek out learning opportunities. Above all, ask ChatGPT or Google and make sure you understand the nuances of each of these Pro*** Management roles. Best yet? Ask a mentor who's been there and has done that! *#ShamelessPlug*

Bonus: Portfolio Managers

There is one other category of Pro*** Managers out there. It's a rare, elusive, less-known breed: Portfolio Managers. I have never come across one myself, but I know they exist and, simply put, they manage a collection of Programs. They oversee the prioritisation and resource allocation across multiple initiatives to ensure they collectively meet organisational goals. They balance the competing demands of various programs and projects, making decisions about which initiatives to pursue, pause, or stop entirely based on their alignment with strategic objectives and their potential return on investment.

While Program Managers focus on the strategic execution of specific programs and Product Managers on the lifecycle of particular products, Portfolio Managers ensure that all these efforts are harmonised and aligned with the overarching strategy of the organisation.

If you know one, or are one yourself, hit me up. Would love to learn more about the intricacies of real-life, zero-bullsh*t portfolio management too!

Bonus: Real-life Program and Product Management

To illustrate how Program Managers and Product Managers work together, I'll delve into a real-life example from my time at Amazon Shipping redesigning the way we offered support to shippers. In Amazon Shipping, my team and I owned everything related to Customer Experience and Customer Support from a programmatic standpoint. My role was to ensure that our customer support processes and interactions were top-notch, meeting our customers' expectations and needs. To achieve this, I worked closely with a Product Manager who was responsible for the delivery of new technical products within the Customer Support space. Here's how our collaboration typically unfolded:

Strategic Planning

- Program Manager (me): I would define the long-term plan for customer support. This involved setting high-level goals, identifying key areas for improvement, and outlining the desired future state of our customer support operations. In our case, we wanted to move to a case management and contact routing type of solution to ensure contacts would be handled by the most suitable team/person. Our ultimate goal was to reduce the back and forth between customer and customer support, and improve the overall experience.
- Product Manager: Using the strategic plan I provided, the Product Manager would develop a product vision to achieve those goals. They would identify specific product features and enhancements needed to realise the future state we envisioned. To do so, they would explore existing product solutions (i.e. what software did other parts of Amazon use to do what we wanted to do? What features did they have/not have?), investigate what the market had to offer, or draw from their previous experience working with technical development teams.

Execution

- Program Manager: Once the strategy was approved, I had to coordinate the overall execution of the plan, ensuring that

all projects and initiatives aligned with our strategic objectives. This involved regular check-ins with various teams, managing timelines, and ensuring that all aspects of the customer experience were being addressed. My role also entailed answering product questions (i.e. can we tweak feature X in so and so way? What happens if we can't deliver feature Y right away, etc.) as roadblocks, constraints, or external forces impact our roadmap.
- Product Manager: At the same time, the Product Manager worked with software engineering and various other tech teams to build and launch the required product features. They managed the technical aspects of product delivery, from initial development through to deployment and post-launch support. This also included UAT and QA phases, which were conducted in partnership with me and my team as the Program owners.

Monitoring and Adjusting

- Program Manager: Upon launch, my job was to monitor and audit the performance of the customer support operations using metrics and KPIs to track progress against our goals. If we identified any issues or areas needing adjustment, I would work with the Product Manager to address them.
- Product Manager: Based on feedback and performance data, the Product Manager made iterative improvements to the product, ensuring that it continued to meet the evolving needs of our customers and our strategic objectives.

Communication

- Program Manager: I ensured that all stakeholders were kept informed about the progress and outcomes of our initiatives. This involved regular updates (e.g. weekly summary emails, monthly business reviews, etc.), reports, and presentations to leadership and other key stakeholders.
- Product Manager: The Product Manager communicated with the development teams and other technical stakeholders, ensuring everyone was aligned and aware of their roles and responsibilities. They also owned providing all the product and tech updates when necessary.

Through this collaboration, we were able to create a seamless and effective customer support experience that met our strategic goals and enhanced customer satisfaction. By understanding and leveraging the unique strengths of both roles, organisations can ensure that their Programs and products are not only aligned with strategic objectives but also effectively executed to deliver maximum value to their customers.

A BLUEPRINT FOR REPEATABLE PROGRAM MANAGEMENT

Congrats, you're now a Program Manager. You manage a Program. What Program though? And how do you go about it? Hopefully, your manager will have told you something like: "you're responsible for X Program and I want you to achieve Y by Z date". What if they didn't? Or what if those Xs, Ys, and Zs are still highly ambiguous and not well defined? Or maybe you are just too new to the company to know better.

Easy, we follow the Zero Bullsh*t Program Management **CMM blueprint** which conveniently rests on just three easy-to-remember pillars:

- A **Charter**: The vision, the working tenets, and the strategic plan of action.
- A bunch of **Metrics**: What does success look like and how can it be measured?
- And the right number of **Mechanisms**: After all, "if you can't measure it, you can't manage it".

Truth to be told, while the CMM blueprint provides a solid foundation for program management (and it's an easy and catchy way to remember what to always go back to – charter, metrics and mechanisms), the successful creation and delivery of end-to-end programs requires a more holistic and encompassing approach that extends beyond these three core pillars. As we dive deeper into the next chapter, we will explore additional critical elements that complement and enhance the CMM framework. These include mastering stakeholder management to ensure buy-in and support, conducting pilots to test and refine new initiatives, and implementing thorough post-mortems to learn and improve continuously. My blueprint for repeatable Program Management will develop as follows:

Step 1: **Writing.** This phase of deep and strategic thinking will help you structure and flesh out your programs and initiatives with rigor and intention.

Step 2: **Building**. Everything from mechanisms, to metrics, goals and KPIs, to stakeholder management – all you need to deliver results.

Step 3: Branching out. There is more that awaits you beyond the remits of your program: pilots and experiments, delivering through others, and even building your own PM team.

Step 4: Wrapping up. All things come to end. And you should be prepared for that. Conclude programs effectively, extract valuable lessons, and set the stage for future success.

By integrating these techniques with the CMM blueprint, you'll develop a more comprehensive toolkit that allows you to navigate the complexities of Program Management with confidence and finesse. After all, the goal is not just to manage programs, but to drive meaningful change and deliver tangible (repeatable, awesome) results!

Step 1 - Setting Things Up: The Program's Charter

A charter document is an artefact (a set of slides, a blog post, a manifesto, a list of bullet points, etc.) that helps you define the scope and the goals of your own Program before you start any work. Like any writing, it helps you gain clarity over the breadth and depth of your space and ensure that you're not missing out on any key component before you move on to the execution phase.

Ideally, you want to review your charter with your leadership and obtain their approval before setting anything in motion. This will help you gain exposure and have the executive sponsorship you need to move faster and unlock doors. At the same time, it will allow your leadership team to provide feedback and partake in the decision-making. A win-win, one could say.

For simplicity, we will stick to my favourite type and structure of charter document – the one I learned and perfected over the years at Amazon and what I often go back to whenever I help mentees improve their critical and strategic thinking about their roles, responsibilities, and aspirations at work. You might not need all the sections all the time, and you might also decide to streamline things by removing some of the components. Nonetheless, try to grasp the why behind each section more than the what, and you'll be able to build your own structure as you see fit.

1. Executive Summary

I only really understood how to write actual executive summaries after hearing my manager say something along the lines of: "This section is for the executives in the room. Imagine they were to be pulled out of the meeting five minutes in for something more urgent. This section has to tell them everything the rest of the doc covers in just a few lines". Write this last; it will be much easier, and you'll have a better understanding of what the key points to cover here are. For a real-life example of an executive summary, refer to Appendix 1.

2. Background

Use this section to ground your audience and to ensure everyone understands where you're coming from and where you want to go. Include everything you wish someone had told you when you got started, previous decisions that led the organisation to needing "your program", and anything else in between. Oftentimes, your program is the response to a "problem statement", don't fail to cover that extensively in this section. Watch out for one thing though: this is not a dumping ground and not all the history is actual background. Stick to what makes the most sense in the context of the larger discussion and don't overwhelm the readers. Never lose focus on the objective, even when covering the background. Also, make sure not to introduce concepts or ideas that are not actual background (e.g. don't mention your vision yet).

3. Vision

This is your chance to be bold and to think unconstrained. How do you envision your program? What would you do if you were the most senior person in the room and it was solely your decision? Think big, but be realistic: you don't want the vision to be absurd and unattainable or the audience will lose interest and dismiss your work. The rest of the doc will then help you bridge back to your vision and explain how you plan to get there, what compromises have to be made, or perhaps what investments you would need from your leadership. Until then, use this section to awe your readers and win them over.

4. Guiding principles, tenets

This is where you tell everyone what the rules of the game are and make sure everyone is on-board. You want to be very specific as to what it is that your program will do and not do, and why. And trust me here, it will save you headaches further down the line, especially when dealing with conflicting agendas, internal politics, or constrained resources. For example (more on tenets in Appendix 2):

- We are here to do X and not Y. Example: "The New Sales Motions Program will help the organisation build plug-and-play go-to-market strategies for new customers and new geographies. We will not support existing go-to-market strategies, which will continue to be within the control of local Sales Strategy teams".
- We prioritise X instead of Y. Example: "We always prioritise customer impact over revenue, and long-term

success over short-term gains. When in doubt, we work backwards from the Voice of Customer (VoC) to inform our thinking and prioritise accordingly".

- We operate in X fashion instead of Y. Example: "We index on speed and are willing to take risks if it helps us deliver faster. We are not afraid to fail fast, and we always learn from it. We believe that speed matters and that good enough is better than perfect".

Why is it important to have such guiding principles fleshed out and as public as possible? Because you want to have a way to systematically push back against requests that steer you away from the vision and the plan you laid out for yourself. Next time John Doe comes up and asks you why you're not picking up his requests, you can easily tell him that they don't fit within the working tenets you agreed upon, and that he's welcome to escalate, sponsor resources or otherwise. Done. Bye bye John.

5. Pillars, Big Rocks:

This is where things get more complicated, and way more interesting. Until now, we laid the foundations for our Program and brought everyone up to speed. Our readers should be invested in what we have to say, be clear on why we're saying it, and be excited about our bold and inspiring vision. This is where we hit them with the most thought-out and articulate plan ever. This is where we show them that we are on top of our game and have it all figured out (kind of). To do that, we divide our Program into pillars/big rocks. Careful, I said "Program", not "plan". "Pillars" is different from "milestones". This section is not a tactical and/or chronological plan of action, which will come later. This is where we break down our Program into its fundamental components and, if we are planning on behalf of a team or organisation, where we also explain how we will make use of the headcount we have. If we're not, we will use these big rocks to detail how our own bandwidth will be allocated and consumed going forward.

For example, say we were leading the overhaul of a customer support organisation, and our objective was to reduce customer contacts and the costs associated, our big rocks could look somewhat like:

- **Big Rock 1: Automating internal support and self-service (HC x1).** Today, 20% of the available customer support bandwidth (500 contacts a week, $10,000/month) is absorbed by internal support contacts (employees needing help with corporate travel, their payslips, booking time-off, etc.) since we do not have separate support channels. By documenting the 25 most common contact reasons and producing reliable Standard Operating Procedures, we will allow employees to self-serve 90%+ of all requests, ultimately reducing contacts to ~50/week and cost to $200/month. To do so, we will kick-off a monthly Voice-of-the-Employee session where....
- **Big Rock 2: GenAI for external customer support (HC x2).** In order to not scale Support HC in a linear fashion as the business grows (expected +20% YoY), we will invest in the roll-out of several GenAI applications aimed at preventing contacts before they happen and expediting the resolution whenever contacts do happen.

In H1-24, we will launch MiniGenie, and we will follow up with ContactResolver in H2-24. MiniGenie will consist of intelligent and non-invasive recommendations that will pop-up as our customers browse our website and proceed to check items out. Today most of the contacts have to do with X and by launching MiniGenie we expect to achieve Y...

- **Big Rock 3: Always up-to-date self-service content (HC x1).** Historically, the biggest challenge with static support content is maintaining it up to date and relevant. Going forward we will move the maintenance and the updating of our support content into our recurrent monthly processes. We will give all team members a goal on the number of updated content pages, and inspect progress within local team MBRs. By decentralizing the upkeep, we expect...
- **Big Rock 4: Continuous Improvement (HC x2).** In alignment with the vision to "resolve issues at the core", we will invest in continuous improvement, six-sigma-driven best practices, and we will...

Once the plan is laid out, the only thing our stakeholders will be left wondering will be how we plan to deliver it all, and often, when they can expect to see it all live.

6. Support Needed

You might not always need to delve into a section like this one, but there will be times where your plan will require extra headcount, executive sponsorship, the de-prioritisation of other deliverables, or similar. This is where we think critically about our plan of action and are vocally self-critical with regards to all the dependencies we might have. Often, this section will look somewhat like this: "In order to execute all the big rocks within the expected timelines, we estimate we will require 240 hours from Dev Team A, 120 hours from Marketing Team B, and 80 hours from Enablement Team C. Both Marketing Team B and Enablement Team C can absorb the required workload and are expected to deliver on time. However, Dev Team A only has 180 hours available to allocate to this Program across H1-24. We request that either work X be deprioritised to free up the necessary resources or that leadership allocates Y additional headcount to deliver this Program successfully". Not the most polished sample ever, but hopefully you get the idea.

7. Next Steps

This is where the project management side of things kicks in. Here, we need to take it home and let everyone know that not only do we have a plan to deliver against our vision and our big rocks, but that we will certainly deliver against it. Often, the next steps can be a schematic and concise list (bullet points will do just fine here) of what will happen next, by when and who the owners will be. Just make sure to never miss any of these components (what, when and who). Sticking to our example:

- Create an inventory of most common contact reasons. ETA: Mon-YY, Owner: John Doe.
- Write 25 employee-facing SOPs to allow internal teams to self-serve X categories of issues – ETA: Mon-YY, Owner: John Doe.

- Research third-party GenAI applications and obtain IT and Legal sign-off for internal usage – ETA: Mon-YY, Owner: John Doe.
- Launch of first-ever GenAI application within customer support space – ETA: Mon-YY, Owner: John Doe.
- Identify top 10 recurring customer-facing issues and deploy a mechanism to resolve them at the core, leveraging Six-Sigma and operational excellence best practices - ETA: Mon-YY, Owner: John Doe.

Step 2 - Building: What Success Looks Like

Quick recap – we now have a formalised Program plan and have all the bits and bolts figured out. We have a vision, a strategy to go about it, operating principles, next steps and, if our leadership meetings went well, we should have backing and executive sponsorship too.

Now what? Now we build! We get stuff done! How? Mechanise, Measure, and Manage. Let's go in order.

PS: I lied earlier, the charter document we laid out is not as complete as it should be, but I didn't want to spoil this next section - by far my favourite. In fact, you want to make sure your charter document/artefact also covers what success looks like, especially what goals you will subscribe to and/or what metrics you will track on an ongoing basis. This is important for various reasons, but mostly, it shows the leadership you thought things through at a granular level and that you are on top of it all and ready to execute whilst holding yourself accountable. In practical terms, make sure to always add a section titled "metrics" and/or "mechanisms" after your big rocks and before support needed/next steps. The next few paragraphs will help you understand how to structure it.

Mechanize: Remove Best Intentions

Mechanisms are repeatable processes. They are frameworks that allow teams of any size to function according to established cadences. Monthly business reviews are a mechanism; quarterly board meetings are a mechanism. So are weekly team meetings, daily stand-ups, roundtables, and performance reviews. Mechanisms don't have to be meetings: a recurrent email sent out every X day also functions as a mechanism, as does accessing a KPI dashboard every Monday to inspect your team's performance.

Why are mechanisms so important? They transform intentions into consistent, actionable, and repeatable practices. Relying solely on best intentions leads to inconsistency and oversight, while mechanisms embed rigor and discipline into processes, ensuring that important actions are taken systematically. For example, instead of thinking, "I really want to make sure I let my stakeholders know about the progress every so often", a mechanism would formalise this intention into something like, "I will commit to hosting a project update meeting every Thursday at 2 pm where we go through X, Y, and Z with my key set of stakeholders". This commitment is not left to chance or memory; it becomes a regular, scheduled activity that everyone can rely on.

To me, mechanisms help with:

- **Consistency**: They ensure important tasks and communications happen regularly, reducing the risk of things falling through the cracks.
- **Accountability**: With mechanisms in place, everyone knows what to expect and when, making it easier to hold people accountable for their responsibilities.
- **Efficiency & efficacy:** Mechanisms streamline processes, saving time and effort by reducing the need for ad-hoc decision-making and improvisation.
- **Transparency**: Regular, structured updates and reviews make it easier to track progress and identify issues early, fostering a culture of openness and continuous improvement.
- **Reliability**: Stakeholders can trust that they will be kept informed and that their input will be considered at regular intervals, which helps build trust and confidence in the program.

Now what?

First, clarify to yourself why you need one or more mechanisms. For example, you might want to: offer a 10,000-ft view to a very large set of stakeholders without expecting much from them, go very granular with a core set of colleagues whose deliverables impact the success of your own program, or call out risks and opportunities to ensure leadership is aware and offers support when needed. The reasons for wanting a mechanism are endless, but be very specific upfront so you can design the best solution possible.

Second, build the actual cadence. It might seem obvious, but mechanisms might take a while to bear the fruits you'd hoped for. During the initial phase, remain open-minded and ensure there are ways to collect the voice of your customers: is the mechanism useful to whoever is taking part in it? Can you make changes? Are you focusing on the right things? Etc. Then, stick to the plan. This is by far the most important part of launching and owning a mechanism: consistency. If you decide to send out a weekly email, the email has to go out every week – without fail. If you cannot send it (e.g., you are on business travel, on holiday, on sick leave, etc.) or it does not make sense to send it (e.g., not enough updates since last time), let your stakeholders know in advance.

A blueprint for mechanisms-setting

I built this matrix to help you design the right mix of mechanisms depending on a variety of factors characterising your Program. This is just a guideline, though; feel free to mix and match as you see fit!

For more ideas on mechanisms, have a look at Appendix 3.

Criteria	Light Touch	Medium Touch	Heavy Touch
What	Monthly Email or Monthly Meeting w/ Stakeholders	Weekly Meeting w/ Core Team & Monthly Email w/ Leadership	Weekly Meeting w/ Core Team & Monthly Email or Meeting w/ Leadership & Quarterly Email to Wider Set of Stakeholders
Why	Ideal for less critical initiatives or where the timelines are more flexible.	Ideal for programs backed by leadership but with longer timelines or other high-priority projects.	Ideal for highest stakes programs with high leadership involvement and urgency.
Pros	Low maintenance, easy to manage	Balances regular updates with focused attention	Ensures continuous oversight, prompt issue resolution, high engagement
Cons	Risk of being too infrequent or missing details	Requires consistent effort and coordination	High effort, potential for meeting fatigue
Internal Audience	Broad team, less frequent updates needed	Core team, close collaborators	Core team, leadership, and extended stakeholders
External Audience	External stakeholders needing periodic updates	Key partners and external collaborators	High-impact external stakeholders requiring detailed, frequent updates

A Blueprint for Repeatable Program Management

Measure: Metrics, Goals and KPIs

What's the difference between metrics, goals and key performance indicators (KPIs)? What about objectives & key results (OKRs)? And critical success factors (CSFs)?

A quick 30-second Google search will do a much better job at differentiating them than the next few paragraphs. Fortunately, that's not the purpose of this book, and I am not here to lecture anyone.

At their core, these concepts share a common purpose: they transform abstract intentions into concrete, measurable actions. Well-designed goals, whether met or missed, green or red, realistic or ambitious, serve as a forcing function. They are a compass for your program. They provide clarity, drive action, and offer a framework for evaluating progress. By setting and pursuing targets, program managers gain a deeper understanding of their business landscape. This, in turn, empowers them to make more informed, data-driven decisions.

But let's go in order. **Goals** are the cornerstone of this structured approach. By setting clear and actionable goals, we create a roadmap that guides our efforts and measures our progress. Only once goals are defined (and agreed upon), can we complement them with metrics (aka **KPIs**) to help us audit and report on progress.

How do you design a goal? Goals should be a few things: SMART (Specific, Measurable, Achievable, Relevant, Time-bound), and focused on the inputs.

Specific: What will be achieved? What actions will you take?

Ambiguity is the enemy of progress. For example, the goal "Investigate the drop in sales" is not specific enough. How do you know if you've completed your goal? What counts as investigation and what doesn't? A more *specific* goal would be "Present the root cause for the drop in sales to leadership by Wednesday next week." Here, you know you've hit your goal if you (1) discover the reason and (2) present it to leadership by a certain time.

Measurable: What data will measure the goal?

Measurable goals allow you to define criteria so you know precisely when they are completed. For example, the goal "We will increase sales by the end of the year" is an ambiguous goal. A *measurable* goal is "We will increase sales by X% (from $Y to $Z) by the end of the year". If you are not looking for an improvement but, say, achieving new targets, then you could write "Reach $X in sales by the end of the year".

Achievable: Is the goal doable? Do you have the necessary skills and resources?

Creating goals which you have no chance of meeting will not drive the right behaviour and could demotivate the individuals involved. For example, the goal "Build and launch a new customer-facing application in a new geography by next week" will likely not be achievable. Setting a reasonable time frame which is difficult to achieve but not impossible will drive the right prioritization and resource allocation. More on striking the right balance when setting *achievable* goals in FAQ1.

Relevant: How does the goal align with broader goals? Why is the result important?

Goals do not work in isolation: you need to ensure that you're aligned with your team/org's priorities. If you're leading a program within a broader organization, make sure the goals of your charter align with those set at a higher level. For example, you could target the "launch of a new website in Spanish by EOY", whilst your larger organization could target the "expansion of all existing services to five EMEA Countries (UK, Germany, Spain, Italy, France) by EOY". Ensure your goals are *relevant,* and you'll benefit from greater support, and visibility, all around.

Time-bound: What is the time frame for accomplishing the goal?

Goals need to have a time frame or deadline. Deadlines improve speed of delivery and help to define what success looks like. For example, setting a goal "Launch a new eLearning course on XYZ" could be completed in two months or two years, but when would it be considered successful? Instead, the goal "Launch a new eLearning course on XYZ by 31-Dec-24" is *time-*bound and specifies a successful time frame. Without an end date, there is no urgency or reason to act immediately.

Let's look at one example:

Goal 1: Program A to increase the operating profit by 10% by EOY.

- Specific: yes, it is specific enough. We are targeting one metric and clearly defining what success looks like.
- Measurable: yes, we have a metric that we can measure YoY.
- Achievable: difficult to tell, but let's assume it is.
- Relevant: yes, which company wouldn't want to increase their margins?
- Time-bound: yes, by the *end of the year.*

Goal 2: Program A will increase the average number of Units per Shipment by 50%, in turn reducing Cost of Shipping by 15% by EOY.

- Specific: Yes, even more specific than goal 1.
- Measurable: yes, we have metrics that we can measure and track.
- Achievable: difficult to tell, but let's assume it is.
- Relevant: yes, we can assume so.
- Time-bound: yes, by end of the year

These are two (seemingly) perfectly fine goals. They are both SMART, and appear relevant enough: shareholders would appreciate the attainment of both objectives – especially if you can prove somehow that the second goal will also ultimately increase the operating profit by 10% (that's a discussion for another time).

However, only the second goal **focuses on the inputs** (the number of units per shipment is, for the most part, a controllable variable for a company that ships packages), while the first remains solely focused on outputs (operating margin is the result of several variables at any given point in time). Without delving too deeply into the details of how transportation companies and their costs work, this makes goal #2 far more actionable and measurable than goal #1, and overall a better target for which to hold ourselves accountable.

This focus on inputs over outputs is crucial in program management, just as it is in successful businesses. For instance, during Amazon's rapid growth phase, Jeff Bezos and his team famously focused on what they called "controllable inputs" – price, selection, and convenience – rather than obsessing over final outputs like total sales or profit. By concentrating on these inputs, they could directly influence the company's success on a daily basis.

Does that mean we should never have **output goals**? No. Every program will benefit from having big, bold, output-focused headline goals just as much as having a whole host of input-focused goals. Ultimately, output goals are usually more appealing to leadership and the easiest ones to talk about on an ongoing basis (i.e. "Increase revenue by X" vs "Increase number of customer outreach by X and revenue realization by Y").

A final note: focusing on inputs may not always show immediate results, but it leads to success over time. As a Program Manager, you have much more control over inputs on a daily basis. These might include factors such as the quality of your team's work, the efficiency of your processes, or the strength of your stakeholder relationships. By building habits and mechanisms that excel in these areas, you're setting yourself up for long-term success.

Outputs will happen as long as you focus on and take action on the right inputs!

How do you design a metric?

We should always be frugal when designing goals for our programs, projects, products, or larger organizations. The more goals we have, the less important each goal becomes, making it harder to track progress holistically. However, we can be more abundant with the metrics we design and track within our space, as our ultimate objective is to ensure we cover all leading indicators of our performance. Designing optimal metrics for our programs involves really only two steps: working backwards from the goals (which must be designed first) and iterating as the program evolves and new insights surface to keep them relevant at all times.

For example – let's assume Program A aims to run a series of large-scale events for customers to attend either in person or remotely. The ultimate goal is to reach a higher number of prospect customers than we could solely by relying on 1-to-1 Sales-led engagements. If we had to hypothesize a series of goals to hold ourselves accountable for, these could be:

- Input Goal 1: organize XX large (250+ attendees) in-person events by EOY.
- Input Goal 2: organize XX remote small (<50 attendees) to mid-size (50-to-250 attendees) events by EOY.

- Input Goal 3: invite XX customers (+XX% YoY) across all event sizes by EOY.
- Output Goal 4: drive $XX revenue from customers who joined any of these events by EOY.

As Program Managers, we could easily leave it at that (provided we make them SMART!) and find ways to report on the progress against those goals without additional overhead. However, we know that building metrics against each goal could help us understand our space better, identify opportunities to double down earlier in the game, and course-correct more effectively as we move through the year.

To build that telemetry, we would then proceed goal by goal, and get to something like this.

Input Goal 1: organize XX in-person large events by EOY.
- Metric 1: Average size of *in-person* events (number of customers invited).
- Metric 2: Turn-up ratio for *in-person* events (invited vs show-up)
- Metric 3: Average cost of *in-person* events.
- Metric 4: Working hours needed to organize each *in-person* event.

Input Goal 2: organize XX remote small/mid-size events by EOY.
- Metric 5: Average size of *remote* events.
- Metric 6: Turn-up ratio for *remote* events.
- Metric 7: Average cost of *remote* events.
- Metric 8: Working hours needed to organize each *remote* event.

Input Goal 3: invite at least XX customers in total (+XX% YoY)
- Metric 9: Total number of invites to in-person and remote events of all sizes.
- Metric 10: Total number of customers who showed-up at either event.

Output Goal 4: drive $XXM revenue from customers who joined any of these events by EOY.
- Metric 11: Number of new sales opportunities created 30/60/90 days after each *in-person* event.
- Metric 12: Number of new sales opportunities created 30/60/90 days after each *remote* event.
- Metric 13: Value of new sales opportunities created 30/60/90 days after each in-person event.
- Metric 14: Value of new sales opportunities created 30/60/90 days after each remote event.
- Metric 15: Opportunity-to-revenue conversion rate for each of these event-driven opportunities.

With just a few metrics, we should have full control over the narrative within our program, and we should be able to articulate exactly why the performance vs goal looks the way it does. Brilliant!

Still not convinced? Let's look at a few scenarios:

Scenario A: You've organized enough events and met goals 1 and 2. However, the revenue didn't increase as much as you had hoped, and therefore you missed goal 4.

- If you invited enough customers and also met goal 3, did they actually attend? Luckily, we have a metric for that, and we can easily check if that's the problem. If it is, how do we get customers to actually show up?

- If customers did turn up, then the problems could be with the number of opportunities, their value, or the effectiveness in converting them to revenue - each requiring a different action.

Scenario B: You met goal 4 and realized enough revenue. You also invited enough customers and met goal 3. However, when you look further, you realize you had not organized enough events and missed goals 1 and 2. Depending on the metrics, the takeaway can differ greatly here.

- If the average value of the opportunities is higher than planned, great! Is it because more large customers attended than small/mid-sized? Or is it because the Sales team exceeded expectations? How do we continue this trend next year?

- If the average value of the opportunities is lower than planned, then it means we either hit goal 4 by opening more, lower-value opportunities, or by converting a higher percentage of opportunities. Again, each requiring a different programmatic action.

And there you have it. By understanding the metrics behind our goals, we can fine-tune our strategies and improve our chances of success in future initiatives.

Manage: Stakeholder Management

Who hasn't heard of stakeholder management at least once? No one.

Who has a clear, ready-to-go understanding of what it takes to manage stakeholders? Also no one.

Only joking... but let's try to address that just in case. Stakeholders are individuals who either care about, or have a vested interest in, your project, program, or deliverable in general. They are those who are actively involved with the work necessary for you to deliver against your goals, or have something to either gain or lose as a result of your work. Your leadership, the core Program team, Product Managers, technical developers, internal and external customers are all examples of stakeholders. Thankfully, not all stakeholders are created equal and not all need to be accounted for in the same way.

All the literature I've read about stakeholder management over the years has always converged towards these tips:

- **Map your stakeholders**: Who are they? Are they internal or external stakeholders? Executives, sponsors, or perhaps customers? Etc.
- **Understand what they want**: What are their interests? What does success look like to them? How do they prefer to be kept up to date? What do they need from you?
- **Keep them abreast**: Involve the right stakeholders in the right decision-making, keep them informed.

All fair enough, but also not particularly useful nor immediately actionable if you ask me. For example, how do I keep my manager vs my leadership abreast? Surely not in the same way? And what do I do once I know what each stakeholder group wants from me and my Program? How do I demonstrate that I'm doing what they want/need me to effectively and repeatedly?

Dissecting each of these problem statements would require a more in-depth analysis of each of the actual use cases and stakeholders, and that is not something that can be done effectively in a 1-to-many setting like this one. Instead, consider talking to an experienced mentor if you face issues managing stakeholders and need hands-on, 1-to-1 type of support.

However, something that has helped me over the years and that can effectively be covered here has been developing a robust mental model to drive systematic, repeatable, and appropriate communication across the stakeholders' group, crafting the best possible type of recurrent email updates to address their ever-changing needs and wants.

For all the classical literature, Google is a click away. Alternatively, have a look at Appendix 4.

Deep dive on recurrent email updates

When executed correctly, communication can empower, engage, and align your stakeholders effectively and with limited effort. As a Program Manager, your email updates serve as an essential tool to enhance visibility, maintain accountability, and stimulate motivation among your team and stakeholders. However, structuring emails in Outlook is difficult and not particularly user-friendly (see FAQ 2).

Here are some tips and tricks that can materially change the quality of your email-based newsletters and flash updates:

1. **Use tables**: I usually use tables with one column and many rows to separate sections in my emails (titles, intros, paragraphs, etc.). You'll see why in a second. Once you've structured your table, set its borders to invisible and your email will look neat and professional.
2. **Build a banner**: This might vary from company to company, but my suggestion is to draft something very simple (unless your company has branding that you can leverage). Perhaps consider using Canva or something similar. This will give your email updates consistency and build brand awareness.
3. **Pick your colours and be consistent**: Keep colours to a minimum (and design with colour blindness in mind!). However, colours as well as font characteristics (bold, italic, etc.) can help scan through long texts with ease and convenience.

Then, map out the stakeholders the communication is going to, the level of detail you want to provide, and the frequency. The most common options are:

➢ **High-level update, broad audience**. Ideal for the broadest type of audience. The intent is to keep everyone who might be interested in your Program informed, even those who might not have an actual stake in the program, product, or project). *Appendix 6 for sample Outlook-based email templates.*

Key traits:

- Not the most frequent update (monthly, quarterly, or even less frequent). Could be leveraged when other mechanisms such as Monthly Business Reviews do not exist or might not be feasible.
- Metrics, goals, ETAs, owners, etc. are often not included. They might be good additions and sometimes even necessary, but the update should remain high-level and strategic.

Watch out for:

- Be conscious of the audience: explain things in a way that everyone receiving your email can understand.
- Be clear on the objective: This is meant to be an informative update for those who cannot join more regular cadences. Use it wisely.

> **Medium level of detail, narrower audience.** For a more targeted audience. The intent is to keep your closest stakeholders and their immediate circle (i.e. their managers or their peers) abreast of the progress made in a specific space (whether the whole program, a project, or otherwise). *Appendix 6 for sample Outlook-based email templates.*

Key traits:

- Usually a more frequent type of update (weekly or bi-weekly), but this template could also be used for monthly updates.
- Metrics, goals, ETAs, owners, etc. are often included.
- The update is used to drive actions, flag issues, escalate blockers, celebrate successes, etc.

Watch out for:

- Be conscious of the audience: you can go a level deeper than you would with the broader type of update, but make sure everyone's aware of what is being discussed - especially when it comes to metrics and numbers.

> **High level of detail, narrowest audience**. No detail should be spared with this type of update. Depending on the size of the organisation, seniority, and other circumstances, you might decide to add the managers of those who work with you for visibility purposes (this is a good way to give recognition as well). *Appendix 6 for sample Outlook-based email templates.*

Key traits:

- Usually, a more frequent type of update (weekly or bi-weekly).
- Metrics, goals, ETAs, owners, etc. are often included.
- The update is used to drive actions, flag issues, escalate blockers, celebrate successes, etc.

Watch out for:

- It's easy to get carried away and assume the audience knows everything that's being discussed in these types of updates. After all, you're addressing them to the core stakeholders. However, when new people come in, or when your email is forwarded further out, having a brief section that new readers can refer to for context, material, background is helpful. Consider building a knowledge repository and referencing it at the top/bottom of each update.

Note: If an update is not needed, do let the audience know - send them an email to make sure they know you're skipping the update and that you didn't forget!

If done correctly, recurrent email updates will allow you to manage your stakeholders effectively in a variety of circumstances, and mastering this art will help you nail small and large stakeholder meetings as well.

Pro tip: set yourself a reminder to make sure these updates go out like clockwork! If applicable, invite those who need to contribute to your updates so that they don't forget either, and you don't have to chase anyone.

Other stakeholder management tips and tricks

Unsurprisingly, managing stakeholders involves much more than just email updates, and I would be remiss if I didn't touch on a few crucial tips and tricks I've learned over the years. These extend well beyond Program Management but are fundamental to building strong relationships within and outside your core set of stakeholders.

Advertise your work. Good work doesn't speak for itself, and you cannot assume others will simply "know", "remember", or somehow "be told". Someone once said: "Mediocre people who work loudly outperform great people who work quietly. Is it fair? No. Is it reality? Yes". You need to speak for your own good work and earn the street cred associated with it. After all, we are in the corporate Wild West here, where only the fittest will... get promoted (bit dramatic but it lands the point). Effective self-promotion is a vital aspect of stakeholder management. Regularly updating your team and leadership about your successes, volunteering for visible roles, and participating in cross-functional projects can enhance your exposure. Here's how I go about it:

- **Work louder. Capture and share your wins:** First off, keep a record of all your wins and make sure to do it as they happen, or you will likely forget some. Then, mention your success stories whenever you can (1-to-1s with your manager, team meetings, stakeholder meetings, newsletters, flash updates, etc.). If you lead a team, ask everyone to do the same and use those success stories to give credit to your people and to convey the impact of your team's work. Sharing achievements not only highlights your contributions but also boosts team morale and visibility. Practical takeaway: start writing a 'work diary' right away ("Dear diary, today I finally met my Revenue KPI! What a relief! Want to know how I did it? Well... I upsold X product to Y customer after they had told me 'no' a bunch of times!").

- **Raise your hand. Volunteer for high-visibility initiatives:** Take on roles that increase your visibility within the organisation. Leading cross-functional projects or initiatives can showcase your skills and contributions to a broader audience. Also, they will get you exposure to new stakeholders and help you expand your network. If I look back, most of my promotions coincided with the successful delivery of some difficult, high-stakes, high-visibility, extra-curricular activities. Volunteering for these roles demonstrates your leadership potential and commitment to the organisation, paving the way for career advancement.

- **Find your edge. Build and maintain your own brand:** Find the things you're best at and make sure everyone knows them. For example, I became really good at SQL early on and helped peers debug their code or build complex scripts. Later, I mastered the Amazon way of writing and became the go-to for reviewing and streamlining docs. Whatever your strength, hone it and let it be your social

currency. This will ensure your name is mentioned in discussions even when you're not around, helping you win over stakeholders.
- **Thumbs up, thumbs down. Seek feedback and accolades:** Ask your colleagues and leaders for feedback regularly to help you grow and improve. It's like getting a cheat sheet for your personal development. Don't just stop at feedback, though. Request endorsements or testimonials to highlight your strengths and achievements too. Positive endorsements act as social proof of your capabilities and can boost your professional reputation. By collecting and leveraging this feedback, you increase your visibility and trustworthiness within the organisation, making it easier to manage your stakeholders whilst advancing your career.

Network within and beyond your team. Networking is a crucial aspect of Program management, given the numerous dependencies and cross-functional interactions involved. This is what I do to keep my stakeholders abreast and convert colleagues into sponsors and allies:

- **Regular 1-on-1s and Check-ins:** Schedule regular one-on-one meetings with key stakeholders and team members. These meetings provide an opportunity to build relationships, understand their needs, and address any concerns promptly. There will be times you won't necessarily have an agenda, and that's OK too. Either ask the other party if they prefer to cancel or use the time to chat. Having time to decompress with colleagues we otherwise only spend time discussing work topics is very important, especially in remote or decentralised environments.

- **Cross-functional gathering**: Organise meetings that include members from different departments and/or people outside your close circle. This can help break down silos and foster a collaborative environment. It will also make it easier to find synergies with teams you normally don't work with. Some examples:
  - Quick coffee-chats where participants are paired randomly (30 min, 10 min intervals)
  - Monthly sessions where experts from different organisations evangelise what they're working on
  - Quarterly ask-me-anything roundtables with other leadership-team members, etc. You will be surprised by the number of new collaboration opportunities and new ideas that will stem from sessions like these.
- **Mentorship and coaching Programs**: If your company offers a formal mentorship Program where mentees can be paired with more experienced/more tenured mentors, don't hesitate and jump on it! If it doesn't, or if you want something less formal, organise one yourself. In my current org (100+ people in total), we hosted scrappy but very well-received speed mentoring events twice in the last year, and allowed anyone to volunteer as mentor and/or to register for sessions. Is this strictly stakeholder management? Maybe not, but you could organise sessions with all the stakeholders working on the same program, project, or product, or better yet - with everyone working on similar programs, projects, or products but not yet collaborating enough.

Effective stakeholder management requires ongoing effort, strategic communication, and a proactive approach to relationship building. With these tips and tricks, you'll be well-equipped to navigate the complexities of stakeholder dynamics and drive your projects to success.

Step 3 - Branching Out: Beyond Your Program

Our Program is up and running, we have a good grasp of the rhythm of the business, have implemented mechanisms to help us audit and stay on track and – barring emergencies and escalations – things are running smoothly. Now what?

Now we think big and experiment. We take time to grow our team, if we have one. If not, we double down on our delivery through others to relentlessly push the bounds of our space. In other words: we branch out.

After all, stasis is death. And no one likes slackers either. We can't rest on our laurels. Onwards and upwards!

Pilots & Experiments

One of the things I love the most about running Programs is the ability they give you to think big and bold about the future state of today's space, invent new ways to solve existing problems, and ideate innovative solutions that can positively impact your customers – whoever they are.

Designing and launching pilots to test theories before they become fully-fledged initiatives under the Program's umbrella is the pinnacle of that relentless pursuit to improve the status quo.

Granted, not all companies will foster an environment where trialling new initiatives is encouraged and supported. However, mentoring PMs across the most disparate companies has made me realise that a big part of that resides in how we position the pilot in the first place. The key to running a pilot successfully (which is different to having a successful pilot) is rigour and structure. In fact, the point of experimenting is not necessarily to prove that we are "right" or that our theory is "correct". All we want to achieve with a pilot is to corroborate whether something is worth pursuing further, or not. Demonstrating that the initiative we piloted is not worth scaling is just as good of an outcome – as long as we have learned and collected enough data points throughout the process.

The structure of a pilot. Companies have different ways of approaching pilots/experiments. Some expect Program Managers to fill in or compile some sort of spreadsheet with key data points (objectives, market research, expected results, risk management, financials, etc.), whilst others are a lot less structured and let people carry on as long as there is no direct financial impact (else they would require a sign-off from a finance POC – which can happen via email).

To me, at a fundamental level, you will always need to focus on three things (+ one):

1. **A solid theory to prove**. A/B testing is not the same as running an actual, programmatic pilot – FAQ 3. Both have their place, and A/B testing is just as important. However,

complex motions that need the allocation of existing resources will benefit from the rigour that comes with organising, and running, a pilot beforehand. For example, running a controlled pilot to test a new go-to-market strategy, the expansion to a new customer cohort, an alternative customer support system, or a new marketing strategy will allow the Program Manager to gather all the information needed to scale the efforts further.

2. **The right understanding of what good looks like**. By far the most important, and most difficult, aspect to nail. Are you measuring the right metrics to prove your theory? And are you gathering enough data points to conclude with certainty that what you piloted is worth/not worth pursuing? Common mistakes in this phase include dragging the pilot until the hypothesis is proven correct as well as halting efforts before a "sufficiently significant" period of time has lapsed. As much as I would like to, it's impossible to create a distilled one-size-fits-all standard operating procedure on the back of which Program Managers can be certain not to commit these mistakes. My best advice? Talk to someone who's done it before, or build redundancies into your pilot if you don't know any better. For example: interview your customers upfront to learn what their understanding of success looks like, have your success metrics read and approved by a wide set of stakeholders, and/or run the pilot in increments, thoroughly reassessing the need to continue at the end of each period (e.g. every 2 weeks, every 4 weeks, etc.)

3. **A solid "unhappy path"**. I have seen Program Managers discount the fact that their pilots have real business implications way too often. Especially when the risk of

impacting end customers is concrete, building and socialising to all the stakeholders what the set of motions to deploy is in case the pilot turns out to be unsuccessful is paramount. The simplest way is to build redundancies into the plan (start small and roll out progressively, gather voice of the customer at each step of the way, keep the status quo going until well into the pilot, etc.), and to prepare content to address and/or mitigate the changes introduced during the pilot. Also, if you're piloting a new way of doing something, make sure to not deprecate anything until you know that the new way is the right way.

4. **Bonus: seek the right level of approval and/or sponsorship**. This might seem obvious – but my experience taught me it isn't. Discussing pilot proposals with the wrong audiences and/or with the wrong objective in mind is the easiest way to sabotage new initiatives before they even start. Make sure to map out your stakeholders upfront and seek the backing of those that you will need during the running of the pilot. Fewer headaches later on.

Running the pilot. Once the pilot is approved, resourced, and its performance ready to be tracked, the running very much resembles that of any initiative within the scope of the Program. What I've seen work well over the years is keeping the core team responsible for the execution extremely close and informed every step of the way – especially if the pilot is supposed to be a relatively short stint (a few weeks to a couple of months). Similarly, if the number of people involved in the actual execution of the pilot is high (say you are testing a new sales motion with 50-100 sellers), selecting a smaller group of "champions" or "representatives" (in this example, say 5 to 10 sellers) can help keep a much better pulse on the performance and the effectiveness of the pilot.

1. **Tactical meetings.** Daily or weekly stand-ups/check-in meetings, round-robin discussions, regular business reviews to inspect the metrics, 1:1s with key stakeholders, voice-of-the-customer meetings are all examples of effective and necessary cadences to institute and maintain during the running of a pilot. When combined effectively, these forums will allow one to maintain a 360-degree view of everything that is happening during the execution phase at varying levels of granularity. *Pro tip: have a robust note-taking and project-management system to ensure minutes of the meeting and action items are thorough, always up-to-date, and available to all the stakeholders at all time.*
2. **Leadership meetings.** These are less frequent cadences, but crucial to the success of any strategic initiative. Leverage systematic and regular leadership meetings (monthly is usually enough, or quarterly if timelines are more relaxed) to keep your leaders and sponsors informed of everything that's going well but, more importantly, everything that isn't. To quote... myself (see Fed's Corner 4), "escalating sucks, until it doesn't" and it certainly shouldn't be seen as a defeat – especially when running pilots that require prompt and executive decision-making. *Pro tip: keep your leaders abreast throughout the pilot to avoid having to escalate issues they have never heard of before – and better yet, leverage them to open doors for you when it comes to rolling the initiative out.*
3. **Email status updates.** I have a love and hate relationship with email status updates. A well written, well-structured

update is fundamental for many reasons: it allows you to keep a large number of stakeholders up-to-speed every step of the way, it helps to build "brand awareness" with regards to the initiative we are working on, it showcases our work and creates a record of what it is that we own and are responsible for. It is also a great way to allow others to forward and distribute our piece of communication further out and receive feedback from the readers. It's so easy to get swamped by email status updates left and right and end up not reading any.

Pro tip: once you start, you ought to be consistent and stick to your cadence, or you'll lose trust in the audience. However, know when to stop sending email updates or when to switch things up to renew the interest in, and engagement of, your audience.

4. **Concluding the pilot**. As the pilot draws to a close, we ought to approach its conclusion with the same level of rigor and attention to detail as its inception and execution. After all, concluding a pilot is not merely about ending an experiment - it's about synthesizing the wealth of data and insights gained throughout its duration into actionable outcomes. How to best do it will very much depend on the company you work for, but rule of thumb would be to index on some sort of artifact where all the findings, as well as recommendations, are presented back to all the key stakeholders for a final decision-making on what should come next. This could be a document, an email, a PowerPoint, or otherwise.

Whatever you do, don't forget the conclusion that *'we should not pursue what we piloted'* is **not** at all a failure. Ultimately, that's why we experiment in the first place.

Embracing this mindset fully is what will propel us forward in our path to growth, making us disruptive and bold innovators who are not afraid of failing fast as long as they learn from it. *Onwards and upwards!*

Delivering Through Others

Another way to branch out and increase the bandwidth, scope, and pace of our program is delivering through others. This topic has been one of the most discussed during my mentorship sessions, as well as one of my biggest fears/concerns as I left Finance and ventured further into program management. Managers love to index on "delivering through others" (or lack thereof) when coaching their people, especially with individuals on the cusp of approaching more senior job titles (Senior PM, PM Lead, etc. depending on the company). However, very few can articulate what that *actually* entails and how to go about it successfully.

Two minutes of googling and you're inundated with a lot of barely actionable tips and tricks: '*focus on what others can do*', '*develop the middle*' (?), '*talk more about good performance than bad*', '*have after-action meetings*', and so on. I'm sure there is some truth to each of these, and I don't claim to know any better. However, I do think we can do more here and make it more actionable.

Delivering through others can assume many forms. For Individual Contributors, delivering through others entails delivering through colleagues they have no formal hierarchical/organizational 'authority' over. For People Managers, on the other hand, delivering through others encompasses both their direct reports, as well as colleagues and peers with no formal reporting lines.

To me, there is a silver lining across both, and it comes down to a very simple blueprint:

- **Plan A - Why, What and When**. First, make sure to tell people *why* you are asking them to do what you need them to. Bringing people on-board with the bigger picture will help others feel equal partners in the venture and true contributors. Then, pour all your energy into explaining *what* you expect them to deliver. For more complex deliverables, consider writing everything down so you leave no stone unturned and the person you deliver through has a point of reference. *Note*: you should not cover the *how* as you don't want to cross into micromanagement (applies to people managers and individual contributors). Let people experiment and determine the best way to accomplish what you need to get done. Not only will this motivate them more, but it will allow you to benefit from the expertise, experience or simply, the extra time, that someone who you are delegating something to will have. Lastly, tell them *when* you need it done by. Make sure the timeline is realistic and that everyone is aligned to it. After that, step back and focus on implementing a way to check in on the progress regularly. Think regular 1:1s, team meetings, weekly flash updates, etc.

- **Plan B - (Show them) the How**. Plan B really means plan B. You should only resort to taking things over and "showing them *how* you would have done it" when delivering through others hasn't worked or hasn't brought the results you were hoping for. Granted there are many other ways to address these problems earlier on, for example escalating, especially during the delivery phase if ETAs start to slip, or finding new partnerships if there is an actual skills mismatch. However, demonstrating you can do things yourself can also help you earn long-term trust, if done correctly. In case of peer-to-peer relationships, this can be a powerful and effective way to rise and shine above those that couldn't do what you expected them to whilst coaching and educating them. Use with caution though, especially if you are a people manager! #stayhumble.

To all Individual Contributors: as you think about expanding the scope of your program, progressing your career further and showing leadership skills, having examples that speak to your ability to deliver through peers of yours is paramount. Start small, but flex this muscle with intention and gain confidence over time by applying this simple blueprint.

To all People Managers: delivering through your team members should be somewhat more straightforward for you, but the "How" you go about it is crucial for your own long-term success. Don't end up on the micromanagement end of the spectrum, earn the trust of your people, and make sure you share the grander vision with them at all times. Most importantly, don't be afraid to let things go. You cannot do it all yourself, and you shouldn't.

Building a High-Functioning Team: Beyond The Basics

What best way to branch out and grow our own program than being given a team to hire? After all, forming a team is the natural next step for a successful program that has become too large for one person to manage alone. However, building a cohesive and high-functioning team is a nuanced process that extends beyond hiring the right people. It requires a strategic approach to culture, communication, accountability, and continuous improvement. Not without mistakes, I've learned a great deal over the years and built various teams from the ground-up to address a variety of business needs. This chapter would not be complete without delving into some of the less obvious tips and tricks.

A clarification before we proceed - being a people manager is not, and should not, be a requirement for career advancement. No one should feel pressured into becoming a people manager, and not everyone will want or have the necessary skills (both hard and soft) to excel in this role. And that's OK! Managing others is incredibly rewarding but also taxing and draining, particularly when dealing with issues within the team (performance problems, attitude issues, personal conflicts, etc.). My advice is to start small - perhaps by leading others indirectly or managing interns, apprentices, or graduates. This allows you to gauge your reaction and desire to pursue that path further before committing fully. If you're passionate about it, make sure to talk to your manager and build a career development plan around it.

Now back to my blueprint for building successful teams. For short-term success (1-3 months into building a team), this is what I usually focus on:

1. **Create a shared vision**. To start, every team member should understand and buy into the overarching vision and goals of

the team. To do that, write a comprehensive charter document and treat it as a living artifact, especially in the first 6 to 12 months of operations: revisit it, update it, reshare it, have your team contribute to it as they join and ramp up. This isn't about posting mission statements on the wall and forgetting about them. It's about ongoing, meaningful conversations and regular discussions to ensure everyone understands how each person's work contributes to larger objectives, what the goals are, and what success looks like. Make this a living part of your team's daily work to foster a cohesive and aligned group.
2. **Rigor and structure.** At the start, everything will feel chaotic and uncertain: managers will likely be doing hiring whilst onboarding new members, new hires will not know what to focus on or whom to talk to, and stakeholders will be expecting results sooner than later. That's why it's paramount to establish rigor and structure at the outset. Implement a cadence of daily tactical stand-ups, weekly meetings, and monthly business review sessions. Each meeting should have a clear agenda and objectives, addressing different issues and needs. Leverage daily stand-ups to answer burning questions and ensure your team has a forum to ask questions and communicate with each other (especially if geographically dislocated), weekly meetings for more extensive discussions on work plans and progress, and monthly business reviews for a comprehensive look-back. The sky's the limit when it comes to mechanisms, but remember two rules: don't build too many, and don't wait too long before worrying about structure.
3. **Feedback mechanisms**. Establish channels to collect feedback right away, especially as you're figuring things out

yourself and need to keep the pulse on the rest of your team and the direction you are taking. If soliciting feedback directly doesn't work (rarely worked for me, at least), ask your team to provide their feedback to your manager (their skip) or some other third party (e.g. HR business partner or another manager both you and your team trust) – ideally in some anonymous way. Don't fear feedback and, above all, don't be defensive about it. Your goal should be to build the most cohesive, satisfied, and bought-in team possible. Listen to what they have to say, and you'll get there a lot faster!

My blueprint for medium-term success (3-6 months into building a team):

4. **Goals and KPIs.** If you did your charter right, you should already have defined big rocks and high-level goals for your team. What you might not have immediately are KPIs and more detailed metrics, which is ok. Your team will need some time to ramp up and get the hang of things, as will you. Just make sure not to forget about building measurable indicators of success and auditing them regularly to achieve the best possible results. This isn't about micromanaging anyone; use these metrics to identify areas for improvement and - more importantly - celebrate successes. Also, use these metrics to steer and coach your team from afar, without needing to be involved every step of the way.
5. **Be accessible**. Maintain an open-door policy and be available to support your team. If you have a layered team or a large organization, set up office hours so that people can just turn up. If not, have regular 1:1s and encourage open communication at all times. Ultimately, you are a resource for your team members, and they need to learn when to

leverage you. This approachability helps build strong, trusting relationships.
6. **Recognition and rewards.** Make it a habit to acknowledge and reward both individual and team achievements. This recognition motivates team members and reinforces positive behaviours. Celebrate successes, no matter how small, to build a positive and encouraging team culture.

Lastly, this is what I turn to for more long-term success (9/12+ months into building a team):

7. **Less tactical and more strategic.** Once operations are up and running and your team is formed, make sure to dial-back some of the most tactical mechanisms and processes within the team (e.g. daily stand ups might not be necessary for a program management team). Instead, increase the overall level of autonomy and opt for a more strategic stance to propel things further. For example, think about the year ahead and organize think-big/hackathon sessions to encourage your team to leave their daily routines and spend time brainstorming future plans and big ideas. Look for projects or opportunities outside your immediate organization, and trust some of your team members with stretch projects. Learn what each team member wants to do "when they grow up", be it in 12 months or 5 years, and help them get there.
8. **Professional development**. Invest in your team's growth by providing access to training sessions, workshops, and courses. Encourage team members to pursue continuous learning and skill enhancement - and build individualized plans to ensure everyone does what best aligns with their own needs and aspirations.

Creating and maintaining a high-functioning team is an ever-evolving journey that calls for thoughtful strategy, authentic engagement, and a genuine investment in your team members' growth. When done right, you'll build a team that not only meets but exceeds expectations, paving the way for the long-term success of everyone around (= "a rising tide lifts all boats").

I hope you get to experience the incredible rewards of building such a team in your own career! Now onto the next chapter.

Step 4 - Wrapping Things Up: Happy and Not-So-Happy Endings

Contrary to projects that tend to have expiry dates, Programs often don't and – by design – could run in perpetuity. In reality, they morph, grow, develop and shrink all the time, some might argue a tad too often. There are also times when Programs fail or extinguish their purpose, and documenting their end-of-life becomes as important as articulating everything at the inception.

Importantly, a lot can be learned from pilots, initiatives, or Programs that did not quite meet the mark, whether due to controllable reasons (e.g. insufficient resources, skills mismatch, lack of support, etc.) or uncontrollable ones (e.g. macro-economic changes, force majeure, etc.). Often, the biggest hurdle to overcome is the acknowledgement and acceptance that failing is OK – especially when we do so fast and learn from it. Ultimately, failure is a natural component of innovation and growth, and the result of risk-taking.

Unfortunately, this tends to be the least sexy and often least enforced aspect of any Program Manager's job – but a lot can be sowed from these green fields! All you need is a blueprint to follow.

Happy Endings

Happy endings are what we all strive for in our Programs. They represent the successful achievement of our goals and the positive impact on the business. When a Program concludes on a high note, it's important to celebrate the success, recognise the contributions of the team, and document the best practices and lessons learned. These insights can be invaluable for future Programs and help build a culture of continuous improvement.

Post-mortem. A project post-mortem could either be a retrospective meeting that takes place after a project ends, or similarly to what was covered earlier, a fully-fledged document (i.e. memo, PowerPoint, etc.) to accompany a live review. Program Managers should leverage post-mortems to identify areas of improvement, document lessons learned, and ensure better, more successful outcomes for future initiatives. To insist on the highest standards, they should also ask the working team and/or key business stakeholders to participate in a survey to provide feedback on the program, project or pilot ahead of the meeting, so that the feedback can be collected and compiled beforehand, and the discussion can be as structured and unbiased as possible.

As for the agenda of the meeting, or structure of the document if you so prefer, strive to cover the following key topics:

- **Introduction, purpose**: Set the stage by explaining the purpose of the post-mortem. Ground everyone by talking through the initiative that has since concluded. Emphasise that the goal is to double down on what worked and learn from what didn't, never to assign blame.
- **Review objectives and outcomes:** Once you've outlined the background of the initiative, cover the original goals and objectives, the success criteria that were identified pre-execution, and how the initiative met/didn't meet the expectations. Also cover general, high-level observations. The intent here is to offer a comprehensive overview of the initiative and make sure everyone is on the same page before delving further into the details. Suggestion: make sure to offer a balanced view from the outset and give credit where credit is due. We naturally tend to focus on the negatives more than the positives (negativity bias), don't fall into that trap!
- **Success analysis, highlights**: Identify what went well and why. Discuss the strategies, processes, and actions that led to success. Make sure to unpeel the onion and dig deep into the reasons why things turned out the way they did (same for lowlights, next section). Remember: knowing what worked well will help you inform what to double down on further down the line, increasing your chances of success exponentially.
- **Critical look at challenges, lowlights**: Discuss any challenges faced during the execution phase and how they

were overcome, or not. Highlight innovative solutions and effective problem-solving techniques that surfaced throughout the running of the initiative. Remember: it's OK to fail and make mistakes, as long as we learn from them. Don't sweep dust under the carpet.
- **Lessons learned**: Summarise key takeaways and best practices. Document these insights for future reference. Be thorough and systematic. Think about those who will come after you, or other teams you might want to export your initiative to. This is about building a legacy of continuous improvement.
- **Action plan**: Identify any follow-up actions needed to sustain the success of the initiative and apply the lessons learned to other Programs. Make sure these are clear, actionable, time-bound, and assigned to specific individuals.

Knowledge repository. To maximise the benefits of documenting success, consider creating a knowledge repository where all post-mortem reports and best practices are stored. This repository should be easily accessible to all team members and updated regularly, but it doesn't have to be anything overly complex or time-consuming to maintain: think a Google Drive folder with a bunch of documents within, a collection of internal wiki pages, a Slack thread with links to documents, a Notion template with sub-sections and pages, etc. During my time at Amazon, I've experimented with standard Windows shared folders, online Microsoft SharePoint repositories, as well as with AWS' version of Google Drive: Amazon WorkDocs. Whatever the means of your choosing, here are some of the best practices I've collected through the years:

- **Centralised database**: Use a shared drive where documents are organised by program or project. Think of it as your program management library. This should be the go-to resource for new joiners, anyone looking for more info on previous initiatives, or anyone kick-starting their own program or pilot.
- **Indexing and searchability**: There's nothing more frustrating than having valuable insights buried in a sea of documents. Make it easy for people to find what they need. Ensure documents are well-indexed and easily searchable. Tag them with relevant keywords and categorise them by themes. Harder to set up, but easier to maintain and consume! Look at it as an investment.
- **Regular updates**: Schedule regular updates to the repository to ensure it remains current and relevant. Programs evolve, and so should your documentation. Keep it fresh and up-to-date. If you manage a team of PMs, make it a point to check with your direct reportees whenever new initiatives are either started or concluded.
- **Access and permissions**: Manage access permissions to ensure that sensitive information is protected while still being accessible to those who need it. Balance transparency with security.

By thoroughly celebrating and documenting successful programs, you not only boost team morale but also create a valuable resource for continuous improvement. This structured approach ensures that each program builds on the successes of the previous ones, fostering a culture of excellence within the organisation.

Not-so-Happy Endings

Not every program will end on a high note. Sometimes, despite our best efforts, programs fail to deliver the expected results, or worse yet, are managed poorly throughout with concrete, negative repercussions on either the customer experience, the company's bottom-line, or otherwise. This can be due to various factors, some within our control and some not. The key is always to approach these endings with a mindset focused on learning and growth.

Generally speaking, **post-mortems** are a great way to help crystallize the learnings, but they are usually reserved for initiatives that were executed correctly and according to plan, even if the outcomes might not be as anticipated. However, when a program does not meet its goals and its execution is also questionable, or perhaps something serious, yet unexpected, happens suddenly, it's crucial to understand why and take steps to learn from the experience. Root cause analysis (RCA) is an essential tool in this process. At Amazon, we call this process Correction of Error (COE). RCA involves identifying the underlying causes of problems or failures to prevent their recurrence. It helps to look beyond the immediate symptoms and uncover deeper issues that may have contributed to the failure. Here's how to go about it.

Root Cause Analysis (RCA) is a systematic process used to identify the fundamental reasons for failures or problems. It involves examining the issue at hand, collecting data, and analysing the factors that contributed to the problem. The goal of RCA is not just to fix the immediate issue, but to implement changes that prevent similar problems in the future. There's an abundance of resources online to perfect the art of RCAs but, frankly, it is all fairly boring and very theoretical. Who has ever put together an actual Ishikawa diagram?

To me, the idea of RCA can be boiled down to a few crucial concepts:

- **Identify and define the problem (really well):** What actually happened? Why was that a problem? Are you sure that's the real problem? It's crucial to dig deep and not settle for surface-level issues. Be brutally honest here.
- **Collect data:** Go back to the success metrics and goals you set out to monitor ahead of launch and gather relevant data points to further refine the problem statement. This means looking at all the data, not just the data that supports your assumptions.
- **Identify possible causes:** The Five Whys, a simple but effective tool for identifying root causes by asking "why" five times until the underlying issue is revealed. Make this your go-to RCA methodology, and you'll uncover 80% of the problems with 20% of the effort.
- **Develop solutions:** Brainstorm solutions that address the root causes. Focus on long-term fixes rather than temporary patches. This might involve changing processes, re-training staff, adding redundancies, or even overhauling entire systems.
- **Create an improvement plan:** Implement the solutions. Ensure that there is a clear plan for implementation and that responsibilities are assigned. Without accountability, even the best plans can - and will - fall apart.

- **Monitor effectiveness and follow-up:** After implementing changes, establish a process for monitoring the implementation of the improvement plan. Schedule follow-up meetings to review progress and adjust as needed. This ensures that the solutions are effective and that any necessary tweaks are made.

The ultimate goal of any program, successful or not, should be to drive continuous improvement. Whether celebrating a happy ending or learning from a not-so-happy one, the key is to always move forward with the insights gained. Document everything, share the knowledge, and always strive for better.

Also, be constructive, not destructive. Celebrate wins and state the challenges. Identify where the processes worked well and where they could be improved. Embrace a culture where failure is seen as an opportunity to learn and grow rather than a reason for blame. This approach fosters innovation and resilience, preparing your organization to tackle future challenges head-on.

Remember, every setback is a setup for a comeback. So, take those not-so-happy endings in stride, learn from them, and use them as stepping stones to greater achievements.

GENERATIVE AI FOR PROGRAM MANAGEMENT

As we wrap up our journey through the Zero Bullsh*t Program Management blueprint, it's time to look ahead. Program management, like any field, is constantly evolving. New technologies emerge, methodologies shift, and the skills required to excel are always changing.

One of the most transformative technologies to hit our field in recent years is Generative AI. It's not just a buzzword; it's a tool that's already reshaping how we approach our daily tasks and strategic thinking.

I debated long and hard about where to place this section. Should it be woven throughout the blueprint? Tucked away in Fed's corner? In the end, I decided it deserved its own spotlight, right here before we close things out.

Why? Because understanding and leveraging GenAI could be the difference between being a good Program Manager and a great one in the coming years. It's not about replacing our skills, but augmenting them. It's about staying relevant, being proactive, and embracing the tools that can make us more effective.

So, before we wrap up, let's take a deep dive into the world of Generative AI for Program Management. We'll explore what it is, how it works, and most importantly, how you can use it to supercharge your PM skills.

The Foundations

I committed to not making this book a textbook. However, after hosting sessions for dozens of fellow Amazonians who were curious about the potential of GenAI for Finance and Data Analysis, I understood something. While many of us are familiar with the GenAI buzzwords, the underlying concepts and mechanics remain largely unknown.

I just hope there are no data scientists reading the next few pages. For anyone put off by the oversimplifications, please bear with me or jump to the end. For everyone else, let's demystify some of the jargon together to be more proficient when it comes to leveraging these tools in program management.

Types of Artificial Intelligence

Artificial Intelligence (AI) encompasses a range of techniques and methodologies aimed at enabling computers to perform tasks that usually require human intelligence. Basically, it is the broader concept of machines being able to carry out tasks in a way that we would consider "smart" or "human-like". There are various types of Artificial Intelligence, one of which is Machine Learning.

Machine Learning (ML) focuses on the development of algorithms that enable systems to learn from and make predictions or decisions based on data. Instead of programming every single rule (e.g. if the user clicks that button, then you open that window, if the user scrolls to the bottom of the page, you bounce back up, etc.) we give the machine data (lots of it) and let it figure out patterns on its own (e.g. bunch of photos of cats + bunch of photos of dogs = the ML algorithm can tell which is which when looking at a new photo of either animal).

Now, **Generative AI (GenAI)** is where things get interesting. Unlike other sorts of AI/ML, Generative AI can create new content – text, images, code, you name it. It's not just recognizing, categorizing, or predicting patterns (or is it? we'll get there); it's creating something new. Something that did not even exist in the data it was fed during training. Think of it as the difference between an art critic who can identify painting styles (= tell dogs from cats) and an actual painter who can create new artworks (= painting the image of a cat riding on the back of a dog... whilst walking in space...wearing a cowboy hat. Good thing I'm not a painter.).

Rapid-fire GenAI Jargon

Like any cutting-edge technology, GenAI comes with its own lexicon. Let's demystify some key terms you'll encounter in the AI world to be better equipped going forward.

Large Language Models (LLMs). They're the infrastructure (the big brains) behind customer-facing applications like ChatGPT, Claude, Bard, etc. They are massive neural networks trained on huge amounts of text data. They're also the reason why ChatGPT and the likes sound smart about almost anything.

Transformer-based models. The secret sauce of modern GenAI. First introduced in 2017 by Google researchers, these models excel at understanding context and relationships in text inputs. They significantly improved upon previous architectures, enabling many of the powerful GenAI applications we see today, particularly in natural language processing.

Training. This is what makes or breaks an LLM and what determines its preferred use cases. For example, https://consensus.app is a ChatGPT-like application only trained on academic research to increase accuracy of the outputs and reduce hallucination, whilst ChatGPT was trained using text databases from the internet, which included over 500GB of data obtained from books, web texts, Wikipedia, and other pieces of writing on the internet. It's like sending LLMs to school, but instead of years, it takes weeks (and millions of dollars in compute costs).

Prompting. The art (quite literally) of asking questions to LLMs. Prompts play a critical role in controlling the model's output and the best way of thinking about it is like giving instructions to a very capable, but sometimes quirky, intern. The clearer you are, the better the output. And sometimes, you have to repeat yourself a few times and a few different ways. If you're interested in the art (and science) of prompting, I suggest diving deep on prompting techniques such as chain-of-thought, few-shot learning, fine-tuning, etc.

Tokenization. The process of converting text into smaller units called tokens. The model reads these tokens and uses the relationships between them to understand the meaning and structure of the text. By breaking down the input into tokens, LLMs can effectively learn and generate language patterns.

Attention mechanism. This is a key component of the Transformer architecture that allows the model to weigh different parts of the input based on their importance or relevance to the current context. It's the AI's way of figuring out what's important in a sentence. It's like how you skim a long email but zero in on the parts that matter (like when your boss mentions "urgent"). For example, if I were to say: "I'm Federico, I was born in Italy and therefore I speak…" and let the model finish the sentence, the model would focus its attention on the word "Italy", followed by "I was born", to deduce that the most probable next word in the sentence is "Italian", which is spoken in "Italy".

A Few GenAI Myths To Bust

As with any transformative technology, GenAI has spawned its fair share of misconceptions. Understanding these will help you leverage GenAI more effectively in your work.

Myth 1: "GenAI thinks like humans do"

Reality Check: It doesn't. GenAI is incredibly good at pattern matching and text prediction, but it doesn't "think" or "understand" in any human sense. It's more like an insanely sophisticated autocomplete than a sentient being.

Myth 2: "GenAI is always right"

Reality Check: Nope. GenAI models are predicting the most likely next character in a sentence (Hey, I am Federico and I'm from Italy, therefore I am... Italian? Spanish? English? An Alien? An Accountant? A Program Manager? A Singer?). As fancy and as elaborate as that mechanism can be, it can still result in factually incorrect responses (maybe I am a singer after all?) either because of insufficient or incorrect prompting, or frankly, just because (GenAI is a black box for the most part). Always fact-check crucial information or rely on models specifically designed to limit or reduce hallucinations.

Myth 3: "GenAI will replace human workers"

Reality Check: Not so fast. GenAI is a powerful tool, but it's just that – a tool. It can augment human capabilities, but it can't replace human creativity, emotional intelligence, or complex decision-making. Some argue yet, some argue ever. For the time being, we do have one certainty: GenAI is here to make us more efficient, and we ought to make the most of that and learn how to use it to our advantage.

Myth 4: "GenAI knows everything"

Reality Check: Most GenAI models have a knowledge cutoff date, which is the point up to which data was collected and used for training. If you ask about recent events, you're likely to get outdated or hallucinated information, unless the model can access the web (not all can).

Myth 5: "I can use GenAI for all my work tasks"

Reality Check: While GenAI is versatile, it's not suitable for every task. It shouldn't be used for sensitive data, it can't access your company's private information, and it's not a replacement for human judgment in critical decisions. But we'll explore more of that as we delve further into GenAI for Program Management.

GenAI-augmented Program Management

Think of GenAI as your new super-intern, or millions of interns: incredibly knowledgeable, always available, lightning-fast, but needs supervision and fact-checking.

As anyone who has managed interns - or millions of interns - would know, some tasks might be better suited than others to be allocated to the most junior team members. The same goes with your favourite LLM. Understanding its strengths and weaknesses can supercharge your effectiveness, reduce chances of errors, and make you more productive. Just don't try to fit a square peg in a round hole.

If we think about the typical day-to-day of a Program Manager, GenAI can be really effective at:

- **Summarizing and interrogating large amounts of text**: existing documentation, long email threads, knowledge repositories, etc., GenAI can quickly digest and synthesize information, helping you get to the core of issues faster.
- **Drafting text for us to review and edit further:** think about the strawman of a program's charter document, a

regular email update, a leadership-facing program's update, etc. This can save you valuable time in getting your initial thoughts down, allowing you to focus on refining and personalizing the content.

- **Brainstorming ideas, offering a contrary and unbiased point of view when necessary**: role-playing a think-big idea we have for our program, exploring a contrasting opinion regarding the direction of our initiatives, etc. GenAI can help you break out of your usual thinking patterns and consider new perspectives. Use it as your devil's advocate and you'll be surprised by the results!
- **Analysing data and coding:** debugging Excel formulas, writing SQL or VBA code, drafting quick dashboards, finding patterns in the data, etc. can be drastically accelerated, and democratized, by GenAI. I've hosted a webinar about using GenAI in conjunction with Excel. If you're interested, it's on YouTube: *Generative AI in Data Analysis in Finance Webinar, Federico Maffini.*

But remember, GenAI is just another tool in your toolkit, not a replacement for your expertise. Use it to augment your skills, not to make decisions for you.

- **Use it for first drafts**: let GenAI handle the initial heavy lifting of writing, then refine and personalize the output.
- **Prompt effectively**: the quality of GenAI's output depends on the quality of your input. Learn to craft clear, specific prompts.
- **Respect privacy and security**: never input sensitive or confidential information into public GenAI tools and learn data-handling and GenAI specific policies your company might have.

- **Combine with human expertise**: use GenAI to complement, not replace, human skills like emotional intelligence, complex decision-making, and creativity. Always fact-check important information.

As with any new tool, there's a learning curve to using GenAI effectively. Don't be afraid to experiment, but always apply your critical thinking. Used wisely, GenAI can be a powerful tool in your program management toolkit. Just don't expect it to run your next team-building exercise or smooth over that conflict between marketing and engineering. Some things still need the human touch.

With practice, you'll find the right balance between leveraging AI capabilities and applying your own expertise. *For a glimpse into what your Program Management day-to-day might look like in the near future, have a look at **Appendix 5.** **GenAI-augmented PMs, A Day in the Life.**

CLOSING

And that's all folks! 10+ years of working experience summarized in just a handful of pages. 10+ years of a 9-to-5 life that extends beyond the office hours and creeps into your thoughts 24/7. 10+ years of personal discovery, growth and development. 10+ years of cataloguing successes and defeats, wins and lessons learned. 10+ years of compiling blueprints and playbooks to make future endeavours easier than those before.

At its essence, this is what this book is. The strategies, tips, tricks, and experiences shared in these pages are not meant to be a one-time lesson, but rather a foundation upon which to build your own unique approach to program management. After all, there is no one-size-fits-all solution, and there are plenty of books on program management out there that offer countless directives on how to manage programs or projects. Plenty of theoretical, decades-old insights that readers are left to implement on their own with no guidance and unclear real-life value (been there, done that). And that's where I wanted this book to come in - to be a catalyst for change in that regard.

When I started my journey in program management, I was overwhelmed by the sheer volume of information available. Textbooks, online courses, seminars - they all promised to turn me into a program management guru overnight. But you know what? None of them prepared me for the reality of the job. The late-night emergencies, the stakeholder who just won't budge, the team conflicts that threaten to derail everything - these are the challenges that no textbook can truly prepare you for. That's why I've peppered this book with real-world stories and experiences. Because sometimes, knowing that someone else has been there and survived can be the most valuable lesson of all.

As we've explored throughout this book, program management is a dynamic and ever-evolving field. From setting up a program's charter to navigating the complexities of stakeholder management and beyond, the role of a Program Manager requires adaptability, resilience, and a commitment to continuous growth. Different companies, organizations, and leadership styles will necessarily entail adjustments to the zero bullsh*t program management blueprint. Sometimes, you'll need more bullsh*t than what you'd hoped for (more red tape, more scrutiny, more micro-management). Other times, even less (no documentation, no writing, just doing). And that's fine! Adapt and pivot, but stick to a repeatable blueprint to bring order to ambiguity and chaos.

Now, it would be naïve of me to assume that this book won't be dated in a few years, and it would be equally naïve of you to sacrifice continuous learning. The business world is constantly shifting, with new technologies, methodologies, and best practices emerging all the time. Just look at what AI has done to us in the last 10 to 12 months. So, stay curious and proactive about your own professional development. By doing so, you will ensure that you're always bringing the most value to your teams and organizations.

For example, do you know the many ways GenAI can assist you in your daily PM activities? Or have you researched alternative software/tools to the ones you use all the time? When was the last time you picked up a new skill, wrote something new, built a new process, learned a new Excel formula, created a new report, or spent time with your customers and mapped their needs? *When was the last time you changed the way you did something?*

I'll let you in on a secret: even after all these years, I still make it a point to learn something new every week. Whether it's a new project management tool, a different approach to team motivation, or even just a more efficient way to run meetings - there's always something to learn. And you know what? It keeps the job exciting. It keeps me on my toes. And most importantly, it keeps me growing.

The key takeaway is this: never stop learning and growing. Embrace the journey of continuous development, both personally and professionally. Seek out new challenges, explore emerging technologies, and push yourself beyond your comfort zone. By doing so, you'll not only expand your own skill set but also drive innovation and efficiency within your organization.

Surround yourself with peers, mentors, and mentees who can offer diverse perspectives, challenge your assumptions, and provide guidance and support when needed. Don't be afraid to reach out, collaborate, and learn from others in your field. Embrace failure too. Not every project or initiative will be a resounding success. What matters most is how we learn from and apply the lessons of our failures. By viewing setbacks as opportunities for growth and improvement, we can continue to push ourselves and our teams to new heights.

I can't stress enough how important it is to build a strong professional network. Some of the most valuable lessons I've learned have come from casual conversations with peers, from mentors who pushed me to think differently, and even from mentees who brought fresh perspectives to old problems. And failure? Well, let's just say I've had my fair share. But each failure has been a stepping stone to success, a lesson learned, a story to tell.

As you continue your own program management journey, I hope you'll find the insights and experiences shared here to be a practical, relatable, and inspiring companion, helping you navigate the complexities of program management with greater confidence and success. The world of program management is full of exciting possibilities, and with the right mindset, tools, and support, there's no limit to what you can achieve. Embrace the challenges. Learn from the setbacks. Celebrate the successes along the way.

Remember, program management isn't just about Gantt charts, stakeholder matrices, and risk registers. It's about people. It's about communication. It's about thought leadership. It's about making things happen, often against all odds. It's about those moments when everything comes together, when you see your team's hard work pay off, when you deliver something that truly makes a difference.

Ultimately, your goal should be to build your own version of the **Zero Bullsh*t Program Management blueprint**. When you do so, please reach out and let me know! I'd love to hear and learn from it. Share your own experiences, insights, and lessons learned with me and other readers, fostering a sense of community and collaboration among Program Managers.

And that's really what it's all about, isn't it? Building a community of practice, sharing our knowledge, learning from each other. This book isn't the end of a journey - it's the beginning of a conversation. A conversation that I hope will continue long after you've turned the last page.

Here's to your success as a Program Manager and to the exciting journey ahead! Remember, the best is yet to come. Now go out there and make it happen!

FED'S CORNER

In Fed's Corner, you'll find a curated collection of short articles, personal insights, and thoughts gathered from years of hands-on experience in program management and beyond. This is my space to share unfiltered wisdom, practical advice, and the occasional quirky observation that didn't quite fit into the main chapters. Think of it as an exclusive backstage pass to my professional world – where the lines between consulting, storytelling, and straight talk blur to bring you real, actionable content.

In this section, you'll dive into everything from mastering the STAR interview technique to the art of saying 'no' to your manager, and even the sometimes-uncomfortable necessity of escalation. Each piece is crafted with the same no-nonsense, straightforward style that defines this entire book. Whether you're looking for quick tips to sharpen your skills or deeper reflections to inspire your journey, Fed's Corner has something for you. So, grab a coffee, get comfortable, and let's dig into the nitty-gritty of program management together.

Explore. Learn. Grow.
And remember - zero bullsh*t,
just results.

One
Interview like a STAR

I love interviewing, and I love coaching people on how to prepare for interviews, especially behavioural questions. You can learn so much about someone by hearing them practise for this type of question ("tell me about a time you...") and, if the mentor knows what they're doing, you will often see people blossom in the process.

Mastering behavioural questions is certainly not rocket science, and there's an infinite amount of content online that explains what it means to prepare an answer in a STAR format (Situation, Task, Action, and Results). However, the mentees I have seen go through the most profound metamorphosis often already knew all the theory. What they didn't have was someone there to give them feedback from the interviewer's perspective. Someone who had been on the other side and debriefed hundreds of candidates alongside dozens of other interviewers more (or less) experienced.

As I go back to all my interview-prep mentorship notes, there are a handful of themes that always emerge and that anyone can benefit from knowing and practising:

1. **What you know and what you say are two different things.** Ensuring the person we're explaining our story to understand what we're telling them the same way we have formed the narrative in our head is by far the most difficult aspect of interviewing. Too often have I had to piecemeal stories the candidates were only half-explaining or disrupt

their flow to ensure everything made sense. However, the sooner we realise the other party is NOT privy to all the details we lived through ourselves, the easier for us to address that knowledge gap upfront and interview successfully. To do that, ensure you always level-set with the audience first: start from the beginning, and from a place of assumed ignorance in the other party. Be conscious and intentional about the difference in what you know vs what they know and keep reminding yourself throughout the interview, and especially during the introduction, of that gap. Once the interviewer is equipped with everything they need to understand the rest of your story, move on and take it home.

Tip: If you plan to cover your story in 5 minutes, spend 60 seconds to introduce everything properly.
Trick: Keep the background and intro relevant to the core of the story though. Don't go on a tangent explaining background that has nothing to do with what the question wants you to cover.

2. **Don't lose sight of the track**. It's surprisingly easy to get distracted as we further venture into the response. Thinking on the spot, connecting dots, and following unexplored paths whilst satisfying the unquenchable thirst for information of our interviewer can, and often will, steer us astray. The last thing you want though is hearing the other party say: "Well thank you for covering X, but I was actually asking about Y".

Tip: Jot down the question as they're asking it or, if applicable, ask the question to be written in the chat of whatever online-meeting platform you're using. Then keep that in front of you so you don't deviate from it.

Trick: Quote some of the key words you heard in the question throughout your narrative and link those keywords back to what the company's values, vision, and mission state.

3. **Give me the so-what.** It's too easy to get carried away as we talk through our stories and overly focus on the "How" vs the "What". At the end of the day, if we were having a normal, pub kind-of-conversation with a friend, we would naturally prioritise the parts of the story that would be most captivating and engaging (the "How" more than the "What"). When interviewing though, the opposite is true: the "How" we went about something is important and can help the interviewer understand many important aspects of our persona, but the impact we had (the "What", "So What") or the reason "Why" we did what we did remain of paramount importance.

> *Tip*: Cover the "How" but don't overindulge in it. Instead, be ready to unpeel the "So What" onion several layers deep and talk to your results in detail.
>
> *Trick*: The interviewer will likely leverage your "How" to ask very specific follow-up questions or probe further into what you did. Be ready for that and leverage that to your advantage.

4. **If you struggle to improvise, write it down (but don't recite it!).** Another easy one to address: not everyone can think quickly and improvise great interview responses off

the top. Early on I thought it had to do with being/not being a native speaker, and I mistakenly assumed natives could always improvise and go with the flow during this type of interview. But years of mentoring taught me otherwise: this has very little to do with that and more so with the way we are wired. Also, virtually anyone can benefit from varying degrees of written interview prep. So, don't shy away from that!

Tip: Research the company first and find questions they might ask (Glassdoor, Google, YouTube, even ChatGPT can help there). Then prepare examples for each and write answers down the same way you would if you were interviewing live.

Trick: Don't make the mistake of writing answers down just to read them out loud during the actual interview (seen that many times) as that would not get you very far. Write, rehearse in front of a mirror, and that's it. At most, keep some key words in front of you during the interview, something to help resurface what you have already prepared.

Bonus - work keywords into the answer: a cheeky one, but important nonetheless. Work key words from the job description, the company's values, its mission and/or vision, or other official pieces of content you find online, into your response to win the interviewers over. Extra points if you can make it all sound organic and just the way your brain, work ethic, and attitude really are

Two
Storytelling in Program Management

Storytelling isn't just for campfires and bedtime; it's a powerful tool in the corporate world too. It's how you turn dry data into compelling narratives that inspire, engage, and drive action. Whether you're presenting to stakeholders, writing reports, or mentoring your team, mastering the art of storytelling can significantly enhance your effectiveness and – most importantly – can propel you to new heights: not enough people do storytelling well. Those who can articulate their thoughts clearly, and in an engaging fashion, win audiences over and convince others to jump to action. You ought to master this art.

At its core, storytelling is about making connections. It bridges the gap between numbers and emotions, turning abstract concepts into relatable experiences. When done right, storytelling can help you engage your audience, simplify complex information and ultimately, drive action. After all, people are naturally drawn to stories and are more likely to pay attention, remember details and understand your message when listening to a compelling narration. What is less obvious is that storytelling is as much of a science as it is anything else. Creative writing might not be, but that's not what storytelling translates to in business contexts. As with everything, I have a blueprint for that no ChatGPT could give you.

1. **Prepare the scene**. Typical Who, What, How kind of situation here. First of all, clarify to yourself who your audience is and what relationship you have with them. The

more specific you can be here the better as different audiences will need different types of data, narratives, conclusions and recommendations. Don't be afraid to split your audience into different groups if it can help build more targeted and specific narratives. Then, articulate what you need your audience to do on the back of your story, what data would be best suited to convey your message, and what tone/what level of granularity will be required throughout. Lastly, focus on how you will convey your message to spark the right response, zooming in on the data necessary to make your point across in the most effective and efficient way possible.

2. **Prepare the data**. Finding the most fitting format to display the data we have at hand is the single most impactful activity any (white-collar) storyteller can focus on. We all have a multitude of data points at our disposal and a plethora of data-visualisation tools to draw from, yet 90% of the charts, graphs and PowerPoints we see around us are subpar, confusing and ineffective (I taught a whole class about this earlier in 2023 when I delivered a course on Data Analysis for Finance with ELVTR). In practice though, finding the fitting format is a lot easier than one might assume - it's all about studying a bit of psychology and visual perception (Gestalt Principles of Visual Perception and a list of so-called pre-attentive attributes is all you need here), and practising with Excel.

3. **Prepare the story**. Every good story has a clear structure and you will find most fictional stories follow the hero's journey as their template. However, the weekly business reviews or program charters we all work on don't really have a call to adventure, a supernatural aid, a mentor, a

helper, a villain, a transformation, an atonement, and all that. What our stories need to follow is a simple three-pillar structure that is always, 100% of the time applicable. They need to have a background (setup), a problem statement (conflict) and a recommendation (resolution) – much like Red Riding Hood.
- **Background**: Our Customer Support team lost 2HC in May. Since then, the team struggled to maintain SLA on inbound tickets, which created a backlog of ~35 monthly unhandled tickets.
- **Problem statement**: As a result of the slower turnaround, Customer Satisfaction (CSAT) has been deteriorating (-1.5pts vs May, avg -0.5pts a month) and the number of 1 to 3-star reviews increased 25% in the same period.
- **Recommendation**: To ensure CX does not deteriorate further, we ask our leadership team to release 2xFTEs to backfill currently open reqs as soon as possible.

4. **Deliver the story**. Just like any other skill, storytelling improves with practice. Rehearse your stories until they flow naturally, whether writing (emails, documents) or verbally (leading meetings, hosting forums). If live/in-person, pay attention to your pacing, tone, and body language. If not, learn how your company and your leaders expect you to report news, bridge actuals, present plans, and internalise it. The more you practise, the more confident you'll become.

Storytelling in program management isn't about spinning tales; it's about presenting data and insights in a way that resonates. By turning dry metrics into compelling narratives, you can make your reports and presentations more engaging, memorable, and impactful. So next time you're preparing to share program results, remember: it's not just about what happened, but how you tell the story.

Three
Managers without borders

You will hear haters say managers don't do anything other than delegating so they can sit back and chill. You will hear haters say managers are only interested in their own advancement. You will hear haters say managers are out there to take all the credit for the work of their teams. Reality is you will hear all sorts of takes on management and unfortunately, haters are sometimes right. After all, managing others is tough; it requires a lot of empathy, emotional intelligence and selflessness. It also adds a lot of work to already busy schedules, even when done correctly.

To further exacerbate the challenge, in today's globalised world we will likely find ourselves managing distributed teams. As organisations expand across geographies, managers face the unique challenge of leading teams that are scattered across different time zones and cultures. The lack of face-to-face interaction can lead to miscommunication, decreased collaboration, and a sense of isolation among team members. Navigating these challenges requires a strategic approach and a set of proven practices tailored to the nuances of remote work.

However, there is nothing quite as rewarding as seeing others grow from your advice, trust you as their leader, confide in you, and look to you for support and backup when needed. Managing is not for everyone, and that's OK. It should also not be a prerequisite to career advancement, and no one should feel obligated to do it. But, for those interested or going through the motions – here are some practical tips from my experience with in-person and distributed teams.

A blueprint for managing distributed teams

The first step in managing a distributed team is **understanding your people**. This involves more than just knowing their job titles and responsibilities. It's about recognising their work preferences, energy levels, and personal circumstances. Conducting cultural training exercises to learn about team members' energisers, drainers, passions, and outlets can be incredibly insightful – and it's often a great way to build rapport, camaraderie and break some of those walls. For example, understanding whether someone is a morning person or a night owl can help you schedule meetings and deadlines that align with their peak productivity times while making them feel heard, understood and appreciated.

Once you understand your team, the next step **is to map out the scope of the work**. This means clearly defining the team's objectives, responsibilities, and the profiles required to achieve these goals. Different roles may require different approaches. For instance, business analysts might need more time for independent, focused work, while Project Managers may require frequent interactions with stakeholders.

Mechanisms are the processes and frameworks that remove best intentions and ensure consistency in your team's efforts. These can be both asynchronous (documents, project trackers, shared resources) and synchronous (meetings, brainstorming sessions, rituals). The key is to create an ecosystem of mechanisms that drive accountability and facilitate collaboration, regardless of geographical barriers. For example, after every meeting, ensure that minutes are shared to keep everyone informed and aligned, or expect every person on your team to compile a monthly summary of their highlights, lowlights and key call-outs. In addition, mechanisms can help you ensure and propagate **transparency** across the organisation, which is key to managing any team, but particularly distributed ones.

Setting your team up for success involves establishing clear goals and KPIs – whether your team is distributed or not. This starts with identifying the desired outcomes and working backwards to define the steps needed to achieve them. Goals should be SMART (Specific, Measurable, Achievable, Relevant, Time-bound) and aligned with the overall objectives of the organisation. It's also important to involve your team in the goal-setting process to ensure their personal ambitions are aligned with the team's goals and that everyone feels part of the larger vision.

Beyond achieving immediate business goals, fostering the growth and development of your team members is crucial. **Create personal development plans** in partnership with your team to understand their career aspirations and help them acquire the skills needed to achieve these goals. Whether it's learning new technologies, obtaining certifications, or gaining cross-functional experience, supporting your team's growth leads to higher engagement and better performance.

Managing distributed teams requires a delicate balance of structure and flexibility, and pouring some extra effort into addressing the inherent challenges brought by the lack of physical proximity. By understanding your team, establishing effective mechanisms, setting clear goals, supporting personal development, fostering transparency, and carving out time for personal, non-work-related discussions (think coffee chat sessions, monthly wind-downs, etc.), you can lead your team to success no matter where they are located. In the end, it's about creating an environment where everyone can thrive and contribute to the collective goals of the organisation. Remember, in a world without borders, leadership knows no boundaries. Embrace the diversity, leverage the technology, and lead with empathy and clarity. The world is your office, and your team can achieve greatness from anywhere.

Four
Escalating sucks, until it doesn't

Escalating - the process of moving an issue up the ladder when its resolution surpasses our capability or authority - often feels like a defeat. And when it doesn't, the concern goes toward those we risk to upset.

What if I told you, you too can master the art of escalating?

When to Escalate. Too often, not escalating quickly enough can have disastrous repercussions on the business and its speed. Rule of thumb - if you have exhausted your capabilities or have gone beyond your time frame to handle a situation, it's time to escalate. Try to escalate as late as possible, but still early enough so that the project can be brought back on track. As far as my experience goes, leaders would rather be told sooner than later. Other triggers to look out for?

1. **Risk**: Is the issue likely to result in project delays or budget overruns? Escalate!
2. **Impasse**: Have you reached an impasse where decision-making is stalled, or disagreements have halted progress? Escalate!
3. **Fairness**: Does the issue require you or other team members to work overtime? Does not resolving the issue impact you more than it does others? Escalate!
4. **Authority Limit**: Does the problem require a decision beyond your level of authority? Escalate!

So far so good...

How to Escalate: choosing the right type of escalation. This is where things get tricky, emotional and personal. Most of the people I talked with and mentored throughout the years very rarely failed to appreciate when an escalation was needed. Yet, there is often a common hesitancy to pull the trigger at the right time.

How can we improve this? First off, let's understand which type of escalation applies to us:

1. **Outright Escalations:** The old classic, the "Scorched Earth" approach. This would involve adding both your manager and the other party's manager to an email thread with a candid, albeit often nonconstructive, message along the lines of, "Dear @other party's direct manager, As discussed offline, these are all the reasons why you need to intervene and fix whatever is going wrong with your team member. I have had enough, and I don't want to be thrown under the bus because of them. Thank you byeee". This is the type of escalation you want to avoid at all costs, especially in writing. *Pro tip: if possible, do align with said manager offline and let them resolve the issue with their direct separately.*
2. **Canny Escalations:** A more nuanced and savvy approach, this strategy involves adding a broader group of stakeholders who are likely to support your point of view. The goal here is not necessarily to point fingers, but rather to invite others to weigh in on the issue at hand. Sometimes, you don't even need to add any commentary – a simple "+John, +Josh, +Jade for visibility" at the top of a thread can signal the importance and complexity of the issue at hand.

3. **Forking Escalations**: This method is for the experienced escalators amongst us and requires good relationships with key stakeholders. It involves forwarding the problematic email thread to a senior peer, your manager, or the other party's manager, and continuing the discussion with them privately. The aim here is to reach a decision that can then be cascaded down to the original participants, typically by someone with more authority. This method can help to depersonalise the conflict and bring about a resolution more smoothly.

However, escalating means more than just raising an issue higher up the chain for the more senior leaders to intervene. As a matter of fact, more often than not there isn't even anyone to reprimand. In fact, most escalations are what I call FYI Escalations. These are the kind that require expertise, judgement, business acumen and a highly unbiased, transparent approach to things - even when our "performance" is on the line.

FYI Escalations: the epitome of escalation finesse. These escalations are more about sharing information upwards and sideways rather than resolving an impasse or calling for intervention. FYI Escalations are an invitation for leaders and peers to remain aware of an evolving situation and perhaps provide their insights. This is mostly a proactive way to prevent potential roadblocks or risks from becoming full-blown problems. It requires good judgement to identify what kind of information is crucial and when it should be shared.

Let's consider an example: you're managing a project, and you identify a potential risk that could delay the project. The risk isn't certain yet, but if it materialises, it could impact the schedule. In this case, an **FYI** escalation might involve emailing the key stakeholders, including your manager and the project sponsor, to inform them of the potential risk, your current assessment, and your proposed approach to mitigate it (read that again: "your proposed approach to mitigate it").

FYI escalations can be thought of as strategic communication. They signal that you are in control of the situation, you're keeping an eye on potential issues, and you're involving the right people at the right time. They demonstrate your proactivity and your commitment to transparency, which are both highly valued in professional settings. In many cases, FYI escalations can even help build trust and improve overall communication within the team or organisation.

How to Escalate: the SBAR Format. Regardless of the type of escalation you decide to go for, your communication has to always tick 4 boxes - Situation, Background, Assessment, and Recommendation - without exception. After all, Outlook is not the best vehicle for long-winded rants loaded with emotions.

- **Situation**: Clearly and succinctly describe the situation. What is happening right now that requires escalation? Define the problem and its immediate impact.
- **Background**: Provide relevant information and context. What are the circumstances that led to the situation? Detail any past actions taken, relevant history, or factors contributing to the current issue.
- **Assessment**: Analyse the situation and articulate your understanding of the problem. What do you believe are the

potential consequences if the issue remains unresolved? What are the risks and implications?
- **Recommendation**: Propose a solution or ask for specific assistance. This could include suggesting a course of action, identifying options for the higher authority to consider, or explicitly stating what you need from them.

The **SBAR** framework helps keep communication focused and efficient, and helps to remove biases. With SBAR, your escalation messages will be concise, clear, and actionable, improving the chances of a swift and effective resolution.

In conclusion, escalating doesn't have to be an act of desperation or a sign of defeat. Instead, it can be a tool of empowerment, a display of effective judgement, and a demonstration of your commitment to the success of your project and organisation. It's all about choosing the right kind of escalation, at the right time, in the right way. The more you practise, the more comfortable and skilful you'll become at this nuanced aspect of professional communication. Remember, a well-handled escalation can be a career-enhancer, not a career-ender. So, don't shy away - escalate smartly!

PS: If you're a people manager, one of the most important things you can do is to reward those who escalate appropriately and transparently, no matter how severe the situation. Encourage your team to be vocally self-critical and foster an environment where people feel safe to admit mistakes. You'll reap rich rewards.

Five
Say NO to your manager

What a hard thing to do!

Yet, fostering a culture where it is OK to disagree with your leaders, stakeholders, and/or peers is what has made the most successful companies out there so... successful.

If you are a manager, you have a unique opportunity to encourage a culture of openness and transparency, and your team will look to you for guidance. If you aren't, you can still collaborate with your peers and stakeholders to facilitate a more comfortable environment for disagreement.

Here are some of the things I've observed and learned throughout the years, and some practical tips I've shared with those who asked for my guidance.

The Value of Sparring

Productive conflict, or 'sparring', is essential to team growth. It challenges the status quo, opens the door to innovative ideas, and promotes a learning culture. This isn't about creating discord; it's about encouraging individuals to voice differing perspectives and debate their merits in a respectful, constructive manner.

1. Set **clear expectations**: Let your team know that differing opinions are not just welcome, but encouraged. Provide clear guidelines for respectful debate, emphasising that discussions should focus on the issue, not the person.

2. **Facilitate constructive debates**: Play an active role in directing team discussions. Make sure every voice is heard and that discussions remain constructive and focused on the issue at hand.
3. **Turn sparring into learning opportunities**: After a debate, make time to debrief. Highlight the good points made, where the team landed, and the lessons learned. This will show your team that sparring is a valuable process.

Embracing Failure

Often, the reason why people hold back sharing their ideas and inputs is rooted deeper down. Self-consciousness, the fear of being wrong, and the worry of being dismissed: this is what impedes us from speaking up. But failure isn't a setback - it's a stepping stone. The philosophy of "failing fast" should encourage individuals to take risks, quickly learn from mistakes, and pivot accordingly. As a manager or IC thought leader in your organisation, make sure to:

1. **Promote a safe-to-fail environment**: Encourage risk-taking by emphasising that failure is a natural part of growth and innovation.
2. **Celebrate learning, not just success**: Acknowledge and celebrate the lessons learned from failure. This reinforces that making mistakes is acceptable, as long as we learn from them.
3. **Encourage reflection**: Cultivate a culture of reflection. After a setback, encourage your team (whether your directs or closest stakeholders) to share what went wrong, what they learned, and how they plan to apply these lessons in the future.

Other Practical Considerations

If saying "No" were that easy, I wouldn't have had to coach people through it nor would I be sharing my insights here. Here are a few more inputs to help you get started:

Don't forget to:

- Promote Inclusivity: Ensure all voices are heard, not just the loudest. Create opportunities for everyone to contribute their ideas and opinions.
- Lead by Example: As a manager, your actions set the tone for your team. Demonstrate that it's acceptable to express a divergent opinion by doing so yourself when necessary.
- Demonstrate Respect: Show your team that their opinions are valued and respected. If someone disagrees with you, listen to them and appreciate their willingness to share their point of view.

Practical Tips:

- Train Your Team: Offer training on how to express dissent respectfully and constructively. Equip your team with the skills necessary to effectively communicate their viewpoints.
- Feedback Mechanisms: Establish feedback mechanisms that allow team members to anonymously express their thoughts if they prefer. This can be particularly helpful in the early stages of nurturing this culture.
- Draw the Line: As a manager, there will be times when you need to make the final decision, especially when the team is deadlocked or the debate is not leading to a resolution.

Be sure to explain your decision clearly and reassure your team that their input was appreciated.

Conclusion

As leaders, managers, or peers, we have an opportunity - and a responsibility - to cultivate a working culture where dissent is viewed not as a threat, but as a catalyst for growth. In such a culture, it's okay to say "No," to spar, to fail quickly, and to learn even faster.

This culture demands a shift from focusing solely on outcomes to embracing the process of learning, innovation, and continuous improvement. In this journey, we will encounter disagreement, friction, and failure, but within these experiences lie our greatest opportunities for growth.

FREQUENTLY ASKED QUESTIONS

FAQ 1: How do I strike the right balance between challenging and realistic goals?

Too easy, and you're not pushing your team to their full potential. Too hard, and you risk demoralizing everyone faster than you can say "missed deadline." So, how do we get it just right?

There's this concept in psychology called "Flow" – that state where you're so engrossed in what you're doing that time seems to fly by. It turns out that flow happens when the challenge of the task matches your skill level. Too easy, and you're bored. Too hard, and you're anxious. But hit that sweet spot, and… productivity nirvana!

When we set challenging goals, we're tapping into something called "goal-gradient hypothesis." Basically, people tend to increase their effort as they get closer to a goal. It's like that burst of energy you get when you see the finish line of a race. Challenging goals push people out of their comfort zones, encourage innovation, and can lead to breakthrough performances.

But here's the rub – if goals are perceived as unrealistic or unattainable, it can backfire spectacularly. Decreased motivation, increased stress, and in some cases, unethical behaviour as people try to cut corners to meet impossible targets.

On the flip side, setting goals that are too easy might seem like a safe bet, but it comes with its own set of problems. Sure, you'll probably hit your targets, and there's a temporary morale boost that comes with that. But in the long run, easy goals don't drive growth or innovation. They can lead to complacency and a lack of engagement. It's like only ever lifting the lightest weights at the gym – you might feel good about completing your reps, but you're not getting any stronger.

So, how do we thread this needle?

1. **Start with data:** Look at past performance, industry benchmarks, and your team's capabilities. This gives you a realistic baseline. If you don't have historical (which can often be the case when trailblazing something new), model out all the assumptions of the case, and let everyone know what those are. Seek feedback, adjust where needed, and know when to draw a line in the sand.
2. **Push it (just a bit):** Once you have your baseline, increase the challenge by about 10 to 20%. This is often enough to stretch yourself and your people without breaking anyone.
3. **Break it down**: Big, audacious goals can be overwhelming. Break them into smaller, manageable milestones. This gives your team regular wins (hello, dopamine boost!) while still working towards something challenging.
4. **Involve your team**: Don't just dictate goals from on high. Involve your team, or your stakeholders if you're building goals for your own program, in the goal-setting process.

They often have insights you don't, and they're more likely to buy into goals they helped create.
5. **Provide support**: If you're setting challenging goals for others to deliver, make sure you're also providing the resources and support needed to achieve them. Nothing kills motivation faster than an impossible task with inadequate tools.
6. **Be flexible:** Keep an eye on progress and be willing to adjust goals if needed. Sometimes what seemed realistic in planning turns out to be too easy or too hard in practice. At Amazon, we revisit our "big annual plan" every quarter, and issue revised and updated targets according to how things are panning out. It might not always be applicable, but it's a helpful and effective practice that can be easily exported to program management.
7. **Celebrate progress, not just achievement**: Recognize effort and improvement, not just final outcomes. This keeps motivation high even when stretch goals aren't fully met.

Remember, the perfect balance will vary depending on your team, your program, and your organizational culture. It's not about finding a universal "right" level of challenge – it's about finding the right level for your specific situation.

And here's a final thought to chew on: sometimes, the most motivating goals aren't about numbers or deliverables at all, but about impact and meaning. Why are we doing this program? Who are we helping? What difference are we making? Connect your goals to these bigger questions, and you might find your team pushing themselves harder than any KPI could motivate them to do.

Balancing challenging and realistic goals is more art than science. It requires a deep understanding of your team, your program, and the broader context you're operating in. But get it right, and you'll create an environment where people are stretched but not stressed, challenged but not overwhelmed. And that is where the magic happens.

FAQ 2. What alternatives do I have to Outlook email updates?

While Outlook email updates are a common way to keep stakeholders informed, there are several alternatives you can consider, depending on your company's culture and preferences:

- **Shared documents**: Tools like Google Docs, Confluence, or SharePoint allow you to create and share documents that can be easily updated and accessed by all relevant stakeholders.
- **Project management software**: Platforms like Asana, Trello, or Jira provide a centralized space to track progress, share updates, and collaborate with your team.
- **Instant messaging**: For quick, informal updates, consider using tools like Slack, Microsoft Teams or similar.
- **Recorded video updates**: Create short video updates to share progress, insights, and next steps with your stakeholders. This can be a more engaging alternative to written updates, and you can easily upload them to private YouTube playlists to keep the cost to zero and the privacy as high as an internal proprietary solution.

Remember to choose the method that best aligns with your team's needs and preferences and ensure that everyone knows where and how to access the information they need.

FAQ 3. What's the difference between A/B testing and running a pilot?

A/B testing and running a pilot are both methods for testing and validating ideas, but they have some key differences:

A/B testing:
- Typically used to test small variations in a product, feature, or process. Think about two versions of the same landing page or two versions of a similar call-to-action copy (e.g. "*hey, read this message and go buy this product*") to test which one converts more customers.
- Often focused on a specific metric or set of metrics (e.g., click-through rates, conversion rates).
- Usually involves randomly splitting users or customers into two or more groups, each exposed to a different version of the item being tested.
- Generally shorter in duration and more narrowly focused compared to pilots.

Pilot:
- Used to test larger-scale initiatives or complex changes before a full rollout.
- Aims to validate the overall feasibility, effectiveness, and potential impact of a new approach or solution.
- Involves a limited, controlled deployment to a subset of users, customers, or teams.
- Typically, longer in duration and more comprehensive in scope compared to A/B tests.

- Requires more planning, coordination, and resources to execute successfully.

In summary, A/B testing is best suited for optimizing specific elements of a product or process, while pilots are better for validating the viability and impact of more significant, strategic changes.

FAQ 4: How do I balance multiple programs simultaneously?

Let's face it, in the real world, you're rarely going to be handed just one neat, tidy initiative to manage. More often than not, you'll find yourself juggling multiple balls in the air, each one a complex project with its own set of stakeholders, timelines, and potential dumpster fires waiting to happen. So, how do you keep all those plates spinning, ensuring your overall program meets the expectations?

First off, **ruthless prioritization**. Not all initiatives are created equal, and you need to be ruthless about where you're spending your time. I like to use a simple matrix: urgency vs. importance. Some problems might be screaming for attention (high urgency) but have relatively low impact (low importance). Don't let these trick you into neglecting the quiet but crucial components of your program.

Next, **lean** into those **mechanisms** we talked about earlier. When you're spread thin, having robust, repeatable processes becomes even more critical. Set up regular check-ins for each program/initiative, and stick to them religiously. This might mean more meetings on your calendar, but trust me, it's better than constantly putting out fires.

Delegation is also key here. This is where delivering through others really pays off. Empower your team members to take ownership of specific aspects of each program. Just make sure you've got clear communication channels in place so you're not left in the dark. For example, I love asking my team, or anyone else executing on my behalf for that matter, to send weekly recap emails every Friday, and I rigorously leverage 1:1s for any more in-depth discussions.

Lastly, don't be afraid to **ask for help**. If you're drowning, speak up. Maybe you need additional resources, or perhaps some programs need to be reprioritized at a higher level. Remember, it's better to raise the flag early than to have multiple programs crash because you were trying to be a superhero. *PS: asking for help can lead to strategic and advantageous conversations too. For example, it was when I built a thorough business case and advocated for more support that I was asked to build the first-ever business analytics team within Amazon Shipping.*

Balancing multiple programs is an art, not a science. You'll get better at it with practice, but don't expect perfection. Some days, you'll feel like a juggling maestro; other days, you'll feel like you're herding cats. That's normal. The key is to stay adaptable, keep communicating, and remember to breathe.

FAQ 5: How do I handle scope creep in a program?

Scope creep, the silent killer of programs everywhere. It's like going to the grocery store for milk and coming home with a cart full of stuff you never knew you "needed".

As is often the case, prevention is better than cure. Make sure you have a rock-solid charter document that clearly defines what is (and isn't) part of your program. Remember those guiding principles and tenets we talked about? They're your first line of defence against scope creep. Use them ruthlessly and don't shy away from quoting them back to your stakeholders and leaders whenever they try to stretch you thin.

But even with the best prevention, some scope creep is almost inevitable. The key is to catch it early and manage it effectively. Set up regular review sessions where you specifically look for any tasks or deliverables that seem to be expanding beyond their original boundaries.

When you do spot scope creep, don't panic. Evaluate it objectively. Sometimes, what looks like scope creep is actually a necessary evolution of the program. The business landscape changes, new information comes to light – it happens. The important thing is to make conscious, informed decisions about whether to incorporate these changes.

If you decide that the new elements are indeed valuable and necessary, it's time to renegotiate. Go back to your stakeholders and clearly articulate what the expanded scope means in terms of timelines, resources, and outcomes. Never, ever quietly absorb additional scope without adjusting expectations accordingly.

For the scope expansions you decide against, learn to say no – firmly but diplomatically. Remember what we said about saying no to your manager? Same principles apply here. Explain the impact of the proposed changes and why they don't align with the program's core objectives.

Lastly, document everything. Keep a change log that tracks all requested changes, their potential impact, and the decisions made about them. This not only helps you manage the current program but also provides valuable insights for future planning.

Handling scope creep is as much about managing people as it is about managing tasks. It requires a mix of clear communication, firm boundaries, and the wisdom to know when flexibility is called for. Master this, and you'll find your programs staying much closer to their intended course.

FAQ 6: What's the best approach for transitioning a successful pilot into a full-scale program?

You've run a killer pilot, and now it's time for the main event. Transitioning from a pilot to a full-scale program is like going from cooking for your family to running a restaurant – same basic idea, but a whole new level of complexity. Let's walk through how to make this leap.

Start by doing a thorough post-mortem on your pilot. What worked well? What didn't? What surprised you? This isn't just about patting yourself on the back – it's about extracting every possible lesson to inform your full-scale rollout.

Next, scale up your planning. Your pilot charter was probably pretty focused, but now you need to think bigger. Revisit every aspect of your charter – vision, goals, metrics, mechanisms – and adjust them for the larger scope. This might mean bringing in new stakeholders, expanding your team, or completely rethinking some of your approaches. What worked for your pilot might not cut it for a fully-fledged program. For example, manual processes that you were fine to put up with for the sake of the pilot (speed matters in business and being scrappy is crucial) might quickly become blockers in the scaling phase. Think carefully about the skills and capabilities you'll need, and start lining up those resources early. This might involve some tough conversations about budgets and headcount – be prepared to make your case.

Communication becomes even more critical in this phase. You need to get buy-in from a wider group of stakeholders, many of whom might not have been involved in the pilot. Craft a compelling narrative about your pilot's success and your vision for the full program.

One common pitfall in this transition is trying to do too much, too fast. Yes, you want to capitalize on the momentum from your pilot, but rushing into full-scale implementation can lead to sloppy execution. Consider a phased rollout approach if appropriate.

APPENDICES

Appendix 1: Writing a good executive summary

An effective executive summary is a crucial component of your program charter, as it provides a high-level overview of your plan and key objectives. To write a compelling executive summary, follow these guidelines:

o **Keep it concise**: Aim for one to two paragraphs, or around 150-300 words.
o **Highlight the key points**: Briefly touch on the background, vision, objectives, and expected outcomes of your program.
o **Focus on the "why"**: Emphasize the strategic importance and potential impact of your program.
o **Use clear, jargon-free language**: Ensure that your summary is easily understandable by a broad audience.
o **Tailor it to your audience**: Consider the priorities and concerns of your executive stakeholders, and frame your summary accordingly.

Here's an example of an executive summary for the customer support overhaul program we discussed earlier. As you can see, it covers every aspect of the charter document (from vision to big rocks, to expected results), in a short and compelling way. Usually, executive summaries have leadership-facing action items too at the end so that the leadership knows what's required of them as they read through the rest of the charter.

"With this document, we propose to stand-up a new Customer Program to optimize our customer support operations, reduce costs, and improve customer satisfaction. By leveraging automation, self-service, and continuous improvement initiatives, we aim to reduce internal support contacts by 90%, saving $9,800 per month, and scale our external support capacity to meet the projected 20% YoY business growth. The program will be executed in phases over the next 12 months, with key milestones including the launch of an AI-powered customer support solution and the implementation of a robust knowledge management system. Successful execution of this program will not only drive operational efficiencies but also position us to deliver exceptional customer experiences as our business continues to grow, in line with the 2025 objectives outlined by Company A's annual plan.

To deliver against our plan, we ask for leadership's support to reprioritize the technical roadmap owned by X Product team and to reallocate 2 full-time resources from X to Y team to deliver against our objectives on time."

Appendix 2: Sample tenets from real-life examples

Here are a few more (redacted) examples of guiding principles or tenets from real-life programs I have encountered throughout my career:

We prioritize solutions that are scalable, reusable, and adaptable to future needs, even if they take longer to build. We aim to build foundational capabilities that can support our long-term growth objectives.

- The tenet offers a clear view of the team's priorities.
- It also helps customers understand why the team might decline supporting short-term, short-lived, hacky solutions that would distract them from building long-term.

We make decisions based on data and customer insights. When faced with competing priorities, we always put the customer first and use their feedback to guide our actions.

- The tenet is very crisp and concise, and explains how the team will prioritize going forward.
- It also helps the team push back on eventual requests that are not as customer-obsessed or customer-focused.

We foster a culture of experimentation and continuous learning. We encourage our team members to take calculated risks, learn from failures, and share their insights openly.

- This is a more inward-looking tenet that legitimizes and encourages certain actions or behaviours from the members of the team.
- This tenet offers a simple, yet powerful, way for a team leader to shape the culture of their own team.

Appendix 3: Other examples of mechanisms

In addition to the examples provided in the main text, here are a few more mechanisms you can consider implementing in your program:

- **Quarterly planning sessions**: Bring your team together every quarter to review progress, identify key learnings, and plan for the upcoming period.
- **Bi-weekly project showcases**: Have team members take turns presenting their work, sharing successes, and discussing challenges in a supportive forum.
- **Peer feedback sessions**: Encourage team members to share constructive feedback and insights with each other in a structured, facilitated format.
- **Regular stakeholder check-ins**: Schedule recurring meetings or calls with key stakeholders to keep them informed, gather their input, and address any concerns proactively.
- **Hackathons**: Organize annual or bi-annual events to get your organization to think outside the box and foster innovation at the edges.

Remember, the key is to choose mechanisms that best support your program's objectives and team dynamics and to remain open to adapting them as needed over time.

Appendix 4: More on stakeholder management: Stakeholder Mapping

Stakeholder mapping is a powerful tool for identifying, analysing, and prioritizing the individuals and groups who have an interest in or influence over your program. To create a stakeholder map, follow these steps:

1. **Identify your stakeholders**: List out all the individuals, groups, or organizations that could potentially impact or be impacted by your program.
2. **Analyze their interests and influence**: For each stakeholder, consider their level of interest in your program (low, medium, high) and their level of influence or power (low, medium, high).
3. **Plot them on a matrix**: Create a four-quadrant matrix with "Interest" on the x-axis and "Influence" on the y-axis. Place each stakeholder on the matrix based on your assessment.
4. **Develop engagement strategies**: Based on where stakeholders fall on the matrix, define appropriate engagement strategies:
   - High interest, high influence: Closely manage these key players, involving them in decision-making and providing regular, detailed updates.
   - High interest, low influence: Keep these supporters informed and engaged, leveraging their interest to build momentum for your program.
   - Low interest, high influence: Keep these context setters satisfied, providing them with high-level updates and proactively addressing any concerns.

- o Low interest, low influence: Monitor these bystanders, providing them with general information as needed, but focusing your efforts on higher-priority stakeholders.
5. **Regularly review and update**: Stakeholder dynamics can shift over time, so review and update your stakeholder map periodically to ensure your engagement strategies remain relevant and effective.

By systematically mapping and engaging your stakeholders, you can build stronger relationships, anticipate and address potential roadblocks, and ultimately drive better outcomes for your program.

Appendix 5. GenAI-augmented PMs, A Day in the Life

DISCLAIMER: This entire section was drafted by Claude, Anthropic's version of ChatGPT, based on the context and instructions provided. It was reviewed and adjusted by me, but I purposely left it largely untouched. While it aims to reflect real-world program management experiences, it's a simulation and should be viewed as an illustrative example of how AI will soon be used in everyday program management.

This is the prompt I used to kickstart this back and forth on GenAI-augmented Program Management:

"You are an experienced program manager with 10+ years of working experience across the most successful, innovative and ground-breaking companies out there. You have worked on several cross-functional, multi-faceted and complex projects and initiatives, and have contributed to the success of the

companies and teams you've worked with. You are also a skilled technical person, who's knowledgeable about Generative AI and who's leveraged it time and again to augment his productivity. Write a detailed account of how you use GenAI throughout your workday as a senior Program Manager. Include specific examples, challenges you've faced, and how GenAI helped overcome them. Focus on practical applications in areas like stakeholder communication, risk management, and team leadership. Provide actual prompt examples you've used successfully."

And this is everything I got back from Claude:

After a decade in the trenches of program management, I've seen my fair share of tools come and go. But GenAI? It's revolutionized my workflow in ways I never imagined. Let me walk you through how I've integrated it into my daily routine, and trust me, it's not just about asking AI to write emails. It's about amplifying our capabilities as PMs in every aspect of our role.

1. Morning Prep: Cutting Through the Noise

My inbox used to be a nightmare. Now? It's my strategic launchpad for the day. Here's my go-to prompt:

"Analyze the last 50 emails in my inbox. Categorize them by urgency and project. Summarize the three most critical issues requiring my immediate attention. Then, considering my recurring tasks and our quarterly objectives, suggest a prioritized to-do list for today. Highlight any potential conflicts or dependencies between tasks."

This isn't just about summarization. It's about context, prioritization, and strategic alignment. Last month, this approach helped me catch a critical supply chain issue buried in a long email thread. The AI flagged it as high-priority due to its potential impact on our Q3 deliverables. I was able to address it before it became a full-blown crisis, potentially saving us millions in delayed shipments.

But here's the kicker: the AI also noticed a pattern of similar issues cropping up. This prompted me to initiate a comprehensive supply chain audit, which ultimately led to a major process improvement. That's the power of AI-augmented pattern recognition combined with human insight.

2. Stakeholder Communication: Tailoring the Message

Different stakeholders need different levels of detail, and striking the right balance is an art. Here's how I use GenAI to nail this:

"Draft a project status update for our ERP implementation. Create three versions:

1. A detailed update for the project team, including technical challenges and next sprint goals.
2. A high-level summary for the C-suite focusing on budget, timeline, and business impact. Use no more than 5 bullet points and limit to one page.
3. A mid-level update for department heads highlighting changes to their processes and required actions.

Use our standard traffic light system for status indicators. For any 'red' items, provide a brief explanation and mitigation plan."

This saves me hours of rewriting and ensures consistency across communications. Recently, this approach helped me craft a delicate message about project delays due to a major vendor issue. The AI gave me a solid foundation, which I then fine-tuned based on my knowledge of each stakeholder's hot buttons.

But it's not just about crafting messages. I also use GenAI to prepare for tough conversations:

"I have a crucial conversation with the CTO tomorrow about reallocating resources from his priority project to our critical ERP implementation. Draft talking points that:

1. *Acknowledge the importance of his project*
2. *Present data-driven arguments for the reallocation*
3. *Suggest a compromise that could meet both needs*
4. *Anticipate objections and prepare counter arguments"*

This helped me walk into a potentially contentious meeting well-prepared. We ended up finding a creative solution that kept both projects on track.

3. Project Planning: Proactive Risk Management

Risk management isn't just about listing risks. It's about understanding implications and being prepared. Here's my approach:

"For our upcoming cloud migration project:

1. List 15 potential risks, including technical, operational, and business risks.
2. For each risk, provide a probability score (1-5) and impact score (1-5).
3. Suggest mitigation strategies for the top 5 risks.
4. Identify any dependencies between these risks.
5. Draft a risk response plan for the top 3 risks, including trigger events and immediate response actions.
6. Suggest 3 key risk indicators we should monitor throughout the project."

This method once helped me identify a non-obvious risk in a software rollout - a potential conflict with an obscure regulatory requirement in one of our smaller markets. The AI flagged it based on patterns from similar global rollouts in other industries. We were able to address it early, saving us from a compliance nightmare down the line.

But the real value came from the interconnected nature of the analysis. The AI pointed out a dependency between our data migration risk and our staff training risk. This led us to completely restructure our rollout plan, doing a phased implementation that aligned our data migration with our training schedule. The result? One of the smoothest large-scale implementations in our company's history.

4. Meeting Prep and Reporting: Elevating the Conversation

Meetings and reports are where reputations are made or broken. Here's how I leverage GenAI:

"Review the attached minutes from our last three steering committee meetings. Identify recurring themes, unresolved issues, and decisions deferred. Then, draft an agenda for our upcoming meeting that:

1. *Addresses these points*
2. *Advances our project goals as outlined in our charter*
3. *Includes time estimates for each agenda item*
4. *Suggests pre-read materials for each major topic*
5. *Proposes a 'spotlight topic' for a deep-dive discussion*

Include 2-3 thought-provoking questions for each major agenda item to stimulate meaningful discussion."

For reporting:

"Analyze our project KPIs for the last quarter. Draft an executive summary that:

1. *Highlights our top 3 achievements and their business impact*
2. *Addresses our 2 main challenges and their root causes*
3. *Presents 3 forward-looking strategies tied to our project goals*
4. *Suggests 2-3 data visualizations that best represent our progress*

5. *Includes a 'prediction' section that forecasts potential trends or issues for the next quarter based on current data*

Ensure all points are tied back to our overall program objectives and company strategic goals."

This approach transformed our steering committee meetings from status updates to strategic discussions. The thought-provoking questions have been particularly effective in engaging our executive sponsors and driving decisive actions.

As for reports, our CFO recently noted that our project updates were the most insightful in the portfolio. The predictive element has been a game-changer, allowing us to get ahead of issues before they become problems.

5. Problem Solving: Multidimensional Analysis

When you're stuck (and as a PM, that can happen often) a fresh perspective is invaluable. Here's my favorite prompt for complex problems:

"We're considering shifting to a remote-first work model for our development team. Analyze this decision from six perspectives:

1. *Productivity and efficiency*
2. *Team cohesion and culture*
3. *Talent acquisition and retention*
4. *Cost implications (office space, equipment, etc.)*
5. *Project delivery risks and quality control*
6. *Long-term innovation and creativity*

For each perspective:

- *Provide pros and cons*
- *Suggest data points we should collect to make an informed decision*
- *Propose 2-3 strategies to maximize benefits and mitigate drawbacks*
- *Identify potential unintended consequences*
- *Suggest key performance indicators to track if we implement this change*

Finally, synthesize this analysis into a decision matrix that weights each factor based on our company's strategic priorities."

This multi-angle analysis helped us navigate the post-COVID work model transition. The AI's ability to process vast amounts of information and identify non-obvious connections was crucial. For instance, it pointed out a potential link between remote work and increased security risks in our data handling processes - something we hadn't considered.

We ended up with a hybrid model that boosted productivity and employee satisfaction while maintaining our security standards. The decision matrix has since become a template for other complex decisions in our organization.

6. People Management: The Art of Feedback and Development

Even with AI, people management requires a human touch. But AI can help frame the conversation and provide valuable insights:

"I have a high-performing team member, Jane, who's great technically but struggles with cross-team collaboration. Draft an outline for a performance review that:

1. *Acknowledges her technical strengths with specific examples from recent projects*
2. *Addresses the collaboration issue with concrete instances, focusing on impact rather than blame*
3. *Suggests three specific, measurable goals to improve her soft skills over the next quarter*
4. *Proposes a development plan including training, mentoring, and stretch assignments*
5. *Includes open-ended questions to understand Jane's perspective on these issues*
6. *Suggests a 30-60-90-day plan to track progress on the identified areas of improvement*

Also, provide tips on how to deliver this feedback in a constructive, empathetic manner."

This structured approach has helped me turn potentially awkward conversations into productive dialogues. In Jane's case, it helped us uncover that her collaboration issues stemmed from a lack of confidence in non-technical discussions. We put together a tailored development plan that included public speaking training and cross-functional project opportunities.

Six months later, Jane was leading our inter-departmental innovation task force. The AI-generated 30-60-90-day plan was crucial in keeping us both accountable and tracking real progress.

7. End-of-Day Wrap-up: Strategic Reflection

Ending the day right sets you up for success. Here's my wrap-up prompt:

"Review my calendar and notes from today. Then:

1. *Summarize my key accomplishments, any decisions made, and outstanding action items*
2. *Identify any commitments I made to stakeholders and add them to my task list*
3. *Looking at my calendar for tomorrow, suggest a prioritized task list that balances urgent items with important strategic work*
4. *Highlight any potential bottlenecks or conflicts in tomorrow's schedule*
5. *Based on today's events, identify any emerging risks or opportunities for my ongoing projects*
6. *Suggest one strategic or professional development task I should consider for tomorrow*
7. *Provide a motivational quote relevant to my current biggest challenge"*

This practice has been a game-changer for my productivity and strategic thinking. It ensures I never drop the ball on commitments and helps me maintain a strategic focus amidst daily firefighting. The emerging risks identification has been particularly valuable - it's caught several issues early, allowing for proactive management.

The addition of a strategic or professional development task keeps me growing even on the busiest days. And I'll admit, the motivational quote often gives me the boost I need to tackle the next day's challenges.

Remember, GenAI is a powerful tool, but it's not a replacement for your judgment and experience. Use it to enhance your capabilities, not as a crutch. The key is to craft prompts that leverage your context and experience, always filtering the AI's suggestions through your professional lens.

In my decade as a PM, I've learned that success is about asking the right questions and making informed decisions. GenAI helps you do that at scale, providing insights and options you might not have considered. But the final decisions, the stakeholder management, the team leadership – that's all you.

Use AI wisely, and you'll not just manage programs; you'll transform them. You'll free up mental bandwidth from routine tasks to focus on strategic thinking, innovation, and the human aspects of program management that truly drive success.

The future of program management isn't about AI replacing PMs. It's about AI-augmented PMs who can handle greater complexity, make more informed decisions, and drive unprecedented value for their organizations. Are you ready to become one?

Appendix 6. Outlook email templates

Template 1: High Level and broad audience

- Barebone structure using tables in Outlook or similar email providers (or even Microsoft Word):

Header / Banner
Divisor (font size 5/6 to make it smaller)
Block 1
Divisor (font size 5/6 to make it smaller)
Block 2
Divisor (font size 5/6 to make it smaller)
Block 3

- Actual newsletter template, with visible borders to help you build things out and visualize things:

Team ABC Monthly Newsletter *Month-Year*
Team ABC owns initiatives X, Y and Z. This monthly newsletter is for all our stakeholders to remain up to date on the progress and upcoming milestones etc…
Key Updates & Announcements: 1. X 2. Y 3. Z
Ongoing Initiatives:
Initiative A: XXXX Details: Status:
Initiative B: YYYY Details: Status:
Initiative C: ZZZZ Details: Status:
Resources:
- How to get in touch: email alias, intake mechanism, ticketing system, etc. - Team's resource repository: wiki page, SharePoint, or similar. - Anything else (office hours? On-call schedule?)

- Final product: same structure/same table, but with invisible borders and formatted.

Team ABC Monthly Newsletter
Month-Year

Team ABC owns initiatives X, Y and Z. This monthly newsletter is for all our stakeholders to remain up to date on the progress and upcoming milestones etc…

Key Updates & Announcements:
1. X
2. Y
3. Z

Ongoing Initiatives:

Initiative A: XXXX
Details:
Status:

Initiative B: YYYY
Details:
Status:

Initiative C: ZZZZ
Details:
Status:

Resources:

- How to get in touch: email alias, intake mechanism, ticketing system, etc.
- Team's resource repository: wiki page, SharePoint, or similar.
- Anything else (office hours? On-call schedule? Etc)

Template 2: Medium level of detail, narrower audience

- Actual newsletter template, with visible borders to help you build things out and visualize things.
- Note: you can nest a table into one of the rows of your newsletter whenever you have to report actual metrics or goals to report.

Team ABC
Type/purpose of the update (e.g. Leadership Goals Update, Project X Update, etc): Week XX, 202X
Brief 2 liner to summarize what the email is all about so that the audience is all on the same page.
Key Updates   1. X   2. Y   3. Z
Core Part of the Update: List of Goals, most important ongoing initiatives, milestones, etc.
<table><tr><th>#</th><th>Goal Name</th><th>Status</th><th>Commentary</th></tr><tr><td>0</td><td>Goal</td><td>RAG</td><td>Commentary, Owners and Actions.</td></tr><tr><td>1</td><td>Launch 100 new customers by EOY</td><td>Green</td><td>As of Sep, we have launched 90 customers out of a target of 100…</td></tr><tr><td>2</td><td>Launch Project A by October 23</td><td>Green</td><td>As of Sep, ….</td></tr><tr><td>3</td><td>100% completion of Training XYZ</td><td>Amber</td><td>As of Sep, we are behind our target of… and we're doing XYZ to …</td></tr></table>
"Spotlight" and/or "Highlights/Lowlights" and/or "Coming Up" > each with its own sections
Spotlight: for a topic of your choosing that needs immediate attention   **Highlights/Lowlights**   - [Highlight]   - [Highlight]   - [Lowlight]

- [Lowlight]
Coming Up: focus on the most immediate next steps/milestones that the audience has to be aware of. Particularly useful in case of program updates.

Resources:
- How to get in touch: email alias, intake mechanism, ticketing system, etc. - Team's resource repository: wiki page, SharePoint, or similar. - Anything else (office hours? On-call schedule?)

- Final product: same structure/same table, but with invisible borders and formatted.

Team ABC
Type/purpose of the update (e.g. Leadership Goals Update, Project X Update, etc): Week XX, 202X

Brief 2 liner to summarize what the email is all about so that the audience is on the same page.

Key Updates
1. X
2. Y
3. Z

Leadership-level Goals:

#	Goal Name	Status	Commentary
0	Goal	RAG	Commentary, Owners and Actions.
1	Launch 100 new customers by X date	Green	As of Sep, we have launched 90 customers out of a target of 100... and we're doing XYZ to...
2	Launch Project A by Y date	Green	...
3	100% completion of Training XYZ by Z date	Amber	...

Highlights/Lowlights:

- [Highlight]
- [Highlight]
- [Lowlight]
- [Lowlight]

Spotlight

Goal #3, which targets the 100% completion of training XYZ for every company's employee, is currently Amber with high chances of moving to Red by EOM. The reason is X, and Y person is doing Z to fix it. They need A from the leadership.

Coming Up

The Goals team is organizing a mid-year retrospective with lessons learned and feedback gathered from every team owning one of more of our LT goals. We will do XXX by YYY.

Resources:

- How to get in touch: email alias, intake mechanism, ticketing system, etc.
- Team's resource repository: wiki page, SharePoint, or similar.
- Anything else (office hours? On-call schedule?).

Template 3: High level of detail, narrow audience

- Final product: email ready to go, with invisible borders and formatted.

Project NAME / Program NAME
Team ABC
Week XX, 2024

Brief 2 liner to summarize the project and/or the program so that all readers are on the same page and have the right context.

Highlights
1. XXX
2. YYY
3. ZZZ

Lowlights
1. XXX
2. YYY
3. ZZZ

At a Glance

Key Metrics:
- Impressions grew 20% WoW (100 vs 80 PW) as a result of XYZ
- Click through rate remains flat vs PW (20%) and in line with expectations as XYZ.
- Etc.

Upcoming:

#	Upcoming Tasks	Owner	ETA	Status
1	Analysis to show XYZ	@JohnDoe	Wk1	Green
2	Create process flow to do XYZ	@JohnDoe	Wk4	Amber
3	Review UX and approve for production	@JohnDoe	Wk7	Amber
4	Launch customer feature XYZ	@JohnDoe	Wk8	Green

Challenges / Blockers

- Team X has lost Y resource dedicated to UX Design. The team is working to find an interim solution whilst they backfill so that Project A is not impacted... etc

- Need more tech resources to deliver XYZ feature. Ask for the LT:
  ...

[Optional] Completed/Past Tasks

#	Upcoming Tasks	Owner	ETA	Status
1	Hired X HC and ramped them 2 weeks ahead of expected timeline	@JohnDoe	Wk40	Completed
2	Delivered XYZ feature	@JohnDoe	Wk42	Completed
3	A/B tested XYZ	@JohnDoe	Wk43	Completed
4	Launch of new landing page	@JohnDoe	Wk44	Halted

Resources

- Project Tracker (ASANA, Trello, Notion, Monday, etc.)
- Documentation (wiki pages, google docs, etc.)

INDEX

1

1-on-1s · 36, 41, 47, 48

A

A/B Testing · 51, 111, 112
Accountability · 28, 42, 59, 69, 95
Achievable · 31, 32, 33, 34, 96
Action Plan · 17, 23, 24, 66
Adaptability · 12, 81
Advertise your work · 46
Analytical Skills · 11
Anthropic · 122
Artificial Intelligence · 71, 72, 73, 75, 78, 79, 81, 118, 122, 123, 124, 125, 126, 129, 130, 131, 132
Attention Mechanism · 75

B

Background · 20, 45, 65, 87, 92, 101, 117
Big Rocks · 22, 23, 24, 25, 27, 61, 117
Blueprint · 2, 17, 29, 57, 58, 59, 61, 64, 71, 81, 83, 90, 95

C

Canny Escalations · 99
Charter Document · 10, 17, 19, 26, 33, 60, 61, 77, 81, 114, 116, 117, 127
ChatGPT · 12, 73, 74, 89, 90, 122
Claude · 73, 122, 123
CMM blueprint · 17
Communication · 9, 11, 15, 116, 124
Consistency · 28, 29, 42, 95, 125
Critical Success Factors · 31
CSFs · 31
Customer Focus · 8

D

Database · 67
Delegation · 113
Delivering through others · 56, 57, 113
Design a Metric · 36

E

Email Updates · 41, 42, 45, 46, 55, 110
Escalating · 22, 44, 45, 54, 85, 98, 99, 100, 101, 102

Executive Summary · 20, 117, 127

F

Forking Escalations · 100
FYI Escalations · 100

G

Generative AI · 5, 23, 26, 71, 72, 73, 74, 75, 76, 77, 78, 79, 82, 122, 123, 124, 125, 127, 132
Goals · 8, 9, 10, 11, 13, 14, 15, 16, 19, 24, 26, 31, 32, 33, 34, 35, 36, 37, 38, 39, 40, 43, 44, 45, 59, 61, 64, 65, 68, 69, 70, 83, 95, 96, 97, 99, 107, 108, 109, 110, 116, 124, 127, 128, 130
Goals and KPIs · 31, 61
Go-to-Market · 8

H

Happy Endings · 63, 64, 68, 70

I

Influencing Without Authority · 11
Interview · 86

K

Key Performance Indicators · 31, 129
Knowledge Repository · 45, 66
KPIs · 10, 11, 15, 27, 31, 47, 61, 96, 109, 127

L

Large Language Models (LLMs) · 73
Lessons Learned · 64, 66, 80, 83, 84, 104

M

Machine Learning · 72, 73
Managing Distributed Teams · 94, 95
Measurable · 31, 32, 34, 96
Mechanisms · 10, 17, 26, 27, 28, 29, 43, 50, 60, 62, 75, 76, 95, 97, 105, 112, 116, 120
Mechanisms-setting · 29
Meetings · 26, 27, 45, 47, 48, 49, 54, 56, 57, 60, 70, 82, 92, 95, 113, 120, 127, 128
Mentorship · 3, 4, 49, 51, 56, 58, 86, 89, 90, 130
Metrics · 11, 15, 17, 26, 31, 34, 36, 37, 38, 39, 43, 44, 45, 52, 54, 61, 69, 92, 111, 116
Myth · 75, 76, 77

N

Network · 48

O

Objectives & Key Results · 31
OKRs · 31
Outlook Email Updates · 42, 101, 110
Outright Escalations · 99

P

Pillars · 17, 22, 92
Portfolio Manager · 12, 13
Priority Management · 8
Problem-solving · 11
Product Management · 4, 7, 13
Product Manager · 7, 9, 10, 11, 13, 14, 15, 16, 40
Program Management · 2, 2, 3, 5, 6, 7, 11, 17, 46, 56, 62, 71, 72, 77, 79, 80, 81, 83, 90, 109, 122, 123, 132
Program Manager · 2, 5, 6, 7, 9, 10, 11, 13, 14, 15, 17, 37, 42, 51, 52, 56, 64, 71, 72, 76, 77, 81, 82, 84, 123, 128, 132
Programs Pilots · 50, 51, 52, 53, 54, 55, 63, 64, 67, 111, 112, 115, 116
Project Management · 6, 7, 25, 82
Project Manager · 8, 9, 11, 95
Prompting · 74

R

Recognition · 44, 62, 124
Relevant · 31, 33, 34, 96
Reliability · 28
Roadmap Planning · 8
Root Cause Analysis (RCA) · 68, 69
Ruthless Prioritization · 112

S

SBAR Format · 101, 102
Scope creep · 114
Scope Creep · 114, 115
SMART · 31, 34, 37, 96
Specific · 31, 32, 34, 96
Stakeholder Management · 9, 11, 15, 16, 24, 27, 28, 29, 30, 40, 41, 42, 43, 44, 45, 46, 47, 48, 49, 50, 52, 53, 54, 55, 60, 64, 81, 90, 95, 99, 100, 101, 103, 104, 108, 110, 112, 114, 116, 117, 120, 121, 122, 124, 131, 132
STAR · 85, 86
Storytelling · 90, 92
Strategic Planning · 14
Strategic Thinking · 11, 19, 71, 132
Support Needed · 27, 109

T

Technical Understanding · 8
Tenets · 17, 21, 22, 114, 119
The Structure of a Pilot · 51
Time Management · 9
Time-bound · 33, 34, 96
Tips and Tricks · 5, 42, 46, 50, 56, 59
Tokenization · 74
Training · 74
Transformer-based Models · 74
Transparency · 28, 67, 96, 97, 101, 103

U

Unhappy Path · 52

V

Vision · 10, 14, 17, 20, 21, 22, 24, 25, 26, 58, 59, 88, 89, 96, 116, 117

W

What Good Looks Like · 52

Z

Zero Bullsh*t Program Management · 2, 17, 71, 83

Lastly, a massive

thank you

to everyone who contributed to the public writing of this book.

Your comments, suggestions and feedback were invaluable and had a huge impact shaping the final version.

I couldn't have done it without your support and insights.

Federico